IMAGES OF WAR
THE ROYAL AIR FORCE IN THE COLD WAR, 1950–1970

IMAGES OF WAR
THE ROYAL AIR FORCE IN THE COLD WAR, 1950–1970

IAN PROCTOR

Pen & Sword
AVIATION

First published in Great Britain in 2014
and reprinted in 2017 by
Pen & Sword AVIATION
An imprint of
Pen & Sword Books Ltd
47 Church Street
Barnsley, South Yorkshire
S70 2AS

Typeset by Mac Style Ltd, Bridlington, East Yorkshire
Printed and bound in India by Replika Press Pvt. Ltd.

Pen & Sword Books Limited incorporates the imprints of Atlas, Archaeology, Aviation, Discovery, Family
History, Fiction, History, Maritime, Military, Military Classics, Politics, Select, Transport, True Crime, Air
World, Frontline Publishing, Leo Cooper, Remember When, Seaforth Publishing, The Praetorian Press,
Wharncliffe Local History, Wharncliffe Transport, Wharncliffe True Crime and White Owl.

For a complete list of Pen & Sword titles please contact
PEN & SWORD BOOKS LIMITED
47 Church Street, Barnsley, South Yorkshire, S70 2AS, England
E-mail: enquiries@pen-and-sword.co.ok
Website: www.pen-and-sword.co.uk

Contents

Introduction

This book offers a photographic portrait of the Royal Air Force during the early part of the Cold War, specifically the years between 1950 and 1970 when it underwent considerable change in form and function. The remarkable photographs that form the heart of this book provide a fascinating glimpse into a relatively neglected period of aviation history, when the RAF fulfilled its defensive and offensive roles during a time of great political tension.

The featured images come from a single collection of approximately ten thousand photographs held by Imperial War Museums. Created between 1952 and 1969 by the Air Ministry's (later MoD's) Photography and Reproduction Branch (PRB), these images were deposited with the Ministry of Defence's Negative Library and remained largely unknown until transferred to the museum in 2005. Only a small percentage of this series has been published previously. This book contains over 150 of these images, for the first time published together in their original colour.

Formed of small vignettes, documentary and event photography, the collection offers today's audience an insight into the Cold War duties and day-to-day activities of the RAF. Though there are the expected depictions of royal and military dignitaries and key historical events, the focus throughout is on the work of the 'ordinary' serviceman and woman.

Created as public relations images, these photographs were used by the RAF and the Central Office of Information, appearing in aviation periodicals and newspaper supplements illustrating the work of the RAF. Mostly they featured in brochures aiming to encourage recruitment into a particular branch or trade suffering a shortage of manpower. These two functions have guided the collection's content and the images' style.

The collection's strength lies in the images recording the latest aircraft and the personnel working with them – images intended to inspire boys to become the next generation of aircrew. Similarly prominent are sets depicting the learning and lifestyle available during training at the RAF colleges or at the various schools of technical or administrative training for would-be officers and airmen in skilled, ground-based trades. The recruitment of regular, long-term aircrew and technicians declined sharply at times during the 1950s and 1960s, and the concentration on these subjects is firmly illustrative of the collection's role in recruitment.

The collection affirms the importance of the RAF's day-to-day role at a time when the public was increasingly separated from it, particularly following the abolition of National Service in 1960. To an audience in the 1950s and 1960s, images of armourers 'bombing up' the V-Force, interceptors scrambling or even the aerobatic display teams recreating stylized aerial combat were seemingly familiar. The public memory of the Battle of Britain and the campaign over Germany was still fresh, while those born after 1945 were surrounded by depictions of RAF heroics in the adventure comics and war films of the 1950s. The Ministry's photographs reinforced the message that the RAF of the Cold War, like its Second World War predecessor, was operating confidently as the front line of British defence. At a time when economic uncertainty questioned the RAF's long-term role, communicating this message was important.

By extensively photographing the introduction of new technology and the variety of roles and experiences undertaken by personnel, a valuable resource and a unique social record of the RAF was created. The RAF is presented in a way in which it wished to be seen; confident, modern and relevant. Yet this confidence belies the uncertainty faced by the service. From the late 1950s, regular defence reviews and budgetary cuts substantially affected the role and shape of the RAF, most notably emanating from Minister of Defence Duncan Sandys' infamous 1957 White Paper 'Defence: Outline of Future Policy', which foresaw a massive change in the RAF's priorities and direction.

This book uses the photographs to introduce elements of the RAF's work during the early Cold War period. The chapters have been selected to highlight the strengths of the collection and represents both operational and non-operational aspects. In the front line were squadrons of Fighter, Bomber and Coastal Commands and Second Tactical Air Force (later RAF Germany), along with the ground units supporting them. From 1950, interceptor pilots in Britain and Germany and later tactical nuclear bomber crews, were maintained at a heightened alert state waiting for orders that would signal the start of war. Similarly, the RAF was the first guardian of the UK's nuclear deterrent, perhaps the best remembered of its Cold War roles. For this role, a fleet of highly iconic nuclear bombers and medium-range ballistic missiles was built up, manned by elite air and ground crews. While in Europe the Cold War never turned hot, overseas the RAF was engaged in a number of successive low-intensity campaigns as it withdrew from its stations in the Far East and Middle East. At a time when global travel was still rare, RAF personnel were deployed to some exotic locations in a number of roles, many saw active service.

Several of the British aircraft operated by the RAF have become icons of the Cold War. Yet, frequently pushed to enter service quickly, many of these only reached their potential after successive modifications. Contending with the ramifications from the 1957 White Paper, and a series of budget cuts, the RAF struggled to equip its squadrons with British aircraft. The unclear direction of a rapidly shrinking RAF led to the demotivation of potential recruits and a related reduction in applicants to be aircrew. This compounded a similar problem in the long-term recruitment and retention of technicians required to operate increasingly technical equipment. To the public, the most visible indicators of the changing RAF were the popular display teams, which regularly performed during the 1950s and 1960s. Beyond their value in PR or recruitment these teams served a purpose, but by the mid-1960s their existence was under threat.

The photographs were deposited with the museum with limited accompanying information and understanding this vast collection and its contents is an ongoing process. To get this far, I have had the help of a number of ex-servicemen, too many to name individually, but I would expressly like to thank Peter Symes, Derek Straw, Chris Moreshead, Basil D'Oliviera and Min Larkin who were incredibly patient and polite in response to my many questions about RAF life. I am grateful also to Lee Barton of Air Historical Branch who reviewed the text, and to Ting Baker, who patiently edited it. Naturally, I claim any and all errors or omissions as my own. I would like to thank my colleagues for their endless advice, in particular Alan Wakefield, Ian Carter, Mariusz Gasior and Helen Mavin. My last thanks must go to my parents without whom none of this would have been possible. My late colleague and friend Dave Parry, Senior Curator of Photographs at the IWM, himself a former RAF Telegraphist, encouraged me to investigate this collection and inspired me to produce this book and it is in his memory that this book is dedicated.

HM Queen Elizabeth II's coronation review at RAF Odiham, Hampshire, 15 July 1953. Sizable by later standards, the RAF in the early 1950s was principally equipped with wartime aircraft inadequate for the Cold War. Seen on display are Meteor FR.9s from the Second Tactical Air Force in Germany, Vampire F.3s from Fighter Command and 2TAF, Coastal Command Liberators and Washington B.1s on loan to Bomber Command from the USA. A sign of the future, overhead a flypast of swept-wing Sabres, led by Flight Lieutenant N. A. Burns of 441 Squadron RCAF. In December 1953, 66 Squadron at RAF Linton-on-Ouse became the first of Fighter Command's two stop-gap Sabre squadrons. *(RAF-T 91)*

In one of collection's earliest images, the RAF Regiment parades the Queen's Colour past Buckingham Palace, London, on 17 March 1953, after receiving it from Her Majesty at a ceremony in Hyde Park. Ceremonial events, and the awarding of Colours and Standards, were reintroduced to the RAF during the later stages of the war by King George VI. The Colour, a 3ft 9in square cloth mounted on a pike, is traditionally awarded to units and establishments to recognize service. The RAF Regiment was presented with its colour, the fourth of seven awarded to the RAF, just eleven years after the unit was formed. *(RAF-T 90)*

Wing Commander A. D. Frank and his crew stand near Vulcan B.1 XA896 of 83 Squadron at RAF Waddington, 21 August 1957. This crew was one of the three Vulcans and three Valiant crews selected to represent the RAF at the 1957 Strategic Air Command Bombing Competition at USAF Pinecastle, Florida. Note the aircraft has not yet been painted in the V-Force's more familiar all-white gloss. XA896 was one of the first Vulcans to be delivered to 230 OCU on 7 March 1957, later serving with 83 and 44 Squadrons. In 1964, it was transferred to the Ministry of Aviation to test the engines of the proposed Hawker P.1154 supersonic fighter, and scrapped when the programme was abandoned. With their futuristic designs, the aircraft of the V-Force became symbols of the Cold War. Rather than maintain secrecy, the Air Ministry heavily promoted the custodians of the RAF's nuclear weapons. (RAF-T 335)

Crew of a Victor B(K).1A of 55 Squadron silhouetted against the setting sun at RAF Marham in 1969; the unique shape of the aircraft is instantly recognizable despite the low light. The V-Force formed the RAF's strategic nuclear deterrent from 1956 to 1969, perhaps not coincidentally reflecting the date range in which the majority of these photographs were taken. In May 1965, 55 Squadron, moved from Honington to Marham to become the first of three Victor squadrons operating in the air-to-air refuelling role. It retained this role until 1993, having provided a vital service during the Gulf War. *(RAF-T 8083)*

Senior aircraftmen of 90 (Signals) Group collect their lunch from a dining hall counter on 18 December 1957. Scenes of 'daily life' such as this image feature regularly in the series. Like many such photographs, this image was taken as part of set recording an important event, believed to be a visit to HQ 90 (Signals) Group, RAF Medmenham, by Charles Ian Orr-Ewing, Under Secretary of State for Air, to mark the raising of 90 (Signals) Group to command status as RAF Signals Command in January 1958. *(RAF-T 451)*

Vulcan B.1 XA900 of 230 OCU, seen at RAF Wyton on 28 June 1958 during a visit to the station by HRH the Duke of Edinburgh. On a forty-minute flight to Farnborough, via a simulated nuclear attack on Andover, the Prince took control of the aircraft under the supervision of its captain, Wing Commander Dodd. Also during the Prince's visit was a demonstration scramble by five Valiants of 543 Squadron during which all were airborne within seven minutes. In 1965, XA900 became a training aid at No. 2 School of Technical Training, Cosford, where it was taken over by the RAF Museum and scrapped in 1986. *(RAF-T 653)*

At RAF Horsham St Faith, armourers, under the supervision of a flight sergeant, feed an ammunition belt into one of the two Aden guns mounted in the port wing of a Javelin FAW.4 of 23 Squadron, 25 May 1957. The ammunition appears to be drill rounds. This collection concentrates on aircrew but associated ground-based trades are also well represented. Throughout the period, contemporary recruitment literature emphasized the important role played by all RAF personnel. A 1966 recruitment pamphlet entitled 'Man on the Ground' stated: '*The man on the ground keeps the aircraft in the air. Whatever your trade you'll be in the front line of our defence doing a worthwhile job.*' (RAF-T 284)

Minister of Defence Duncan Sandys is briefed by Squadron Leader Young prior to a flight in Victor B.1 XA937 of 10 Squadron at RAF Cottesmore, 19 June 1959. Sandys' disastrous 1957 Defence White Paper saw a build-up of nuclear forces, such as the V-bombers, as a less expensive form of defence than a large conventional force. It also predicted an end to manned air defence interceptors, cancelling nearly all fighter development programmes and slashing existing air defence squadrons. A 1958 Air Ministry recruitment brochure advised 'You want to fly and, with the RAF, fly you most certainly will ... in some of the world's finest aircraft ... but if you wish to make a fuller career of flying in the RAF, your future will probably lie in bombers, and you can graduate to transport aircraft such as Comets and Britannias.' This vision was ultimately rejected but the effects on the RAF lasted for the next twenty years. (RAF-T 1071)

A pilot climbs into Lightning F.3 XP741 of 111 Squadron at RAF Wattisham, as a member of the ground crew passes to him his Taylor pressure helmet, c. 1965. Reflecting the RAF's pride in the Lightning shortly after its introduction to service in 1960, the Air Ministry made a recruitment film, 'Streaked Lightning' appealing to men who may wish to fly such aircraft. Set to a jazz track the narrator poetically asks: '*Want to fly the Lightning? Want to occupy the single seat, in the single-seater, all-weather, night and day, high-flying, supersonic, super-normal Lightning? Want to fly a Lightning and take you own thunder with you?*' (RAF-T 5759)

At RAF El Adem, near Tobruk, Libya, Pioneers of 230 Squadron, including XL558, are seen following a sortie during Exercise Starlight, March 1960. The aircraft is in front of tents that acted as the squadron's Operations Room and HQ for the exercise. Sets of images, such as this, which record the activities and duties of the RAF's overseas stations, particularly in the RAF's principal bases in Cyprus, Aden and Singapore, are often the only photographs that depict exercises or active operations. *(RAF-T 1710)*

RAF 'At Home' days enabled RAF stations to showcase their work to visiting members of the public. Examples of fighters from the Spitfire to the most recent in service were displayed and flown. At RAF Coltishall's 'At Home' day in September 1960, five aircraft were assembled to mark the 20th anniversary of the Battle of Britain. They were: Hurricane IIc LF363 and Spitfire PRXIXR PM631 (both of the Battle of Britain Memorial Flight), Meteor F.8 WL164, Hunter FGA9 XK136 of 74 Squadron, Javelin FAW.9R XH894 of 23 Squadron and the recently introduced Lightning F.1 XM137 of the Air Fighting Development Squadron, part of the Central Fighter Establishment. *(RAF-T 2087)*

As the youngest of the armed services, the RAF was keen to promote its short yet distinguished heritage. At the parade to mark the disbanding of Fighter Command held at RAF Bentley Priory on 30 April 1968, Air Marshal Sir Frederick Rosier KCB CBE DSO ADC, the last Air Officer Commander-in-Chief (AOCinC) of the command stands with several of the most famous Second World War aces, from left to right: Air Vice Marshal 'Johnny' Johnson CBE DSO** DFC*, Group Captain P. W. Townsend CVO DSO DFC*, Wing Commander R. R. S. Tuck DSO DFC** DFC (US), Air Commodore A. C. Deere OBE DSO DFC* DFC (US) and Group Captain Douglas Bader CBE DSO* DFC*. *(RAF-T 8374)*

Spitfire TE476 and Hurricane LT383 of the Battle of Britain Memorial Flight along with Hunter F.6 XF511 of 43 Squadron and Javelin FAW.7 XH958 of 23 Squadron, in flight in August 1959. The RAF promoted a direct ancestry between the pressure-suited pilots with their modern jet aircraft and 'The Few' with their Spitfires and Hurricanes, whose Second World War actions had gained them an immeasurable public reputation. *(RAF-T 1163)*

Flight Lieutenant Ian Thomson of 111 Squadron stands by a Lightning F.1A at RAF Wattisham, in October 1962. Echoing wartime photography, this image of Thomson is typical of the way RAF pilots are portrayed as the successors to 'The Few'. Flight Lieutenant Thomson served with 111 Squadron from April 1962 until posted to 23 Squadron in June 1964. An excellent sportsman, Thomson represented the RAF at the inter-service lawn tennis championships in July 1962 and also competed with the RAF bobsleigh team at the world championships in Austria in January 1963. *(RAF-T 3498)*

Many of the images are staged or posed, some more noticeably than others, like this image of the air traffic control tower at RAF Lyneham on 26 June 1962. The photographer seemingly controlled the subjects to achieve the most appropriately composed image. Many images depicting aircrew at work inside their aircraft were taken when firmly on the ground. To an experienced audience this staging has made many of the activities recorded inconsistent with day-to-day practice. *(RAF-T 3383)*

Major Yuri Gagarin, the first man in space, is photographed at a reception held in his honour by the Air Ministry on 13 July 1961, during a visit to the UK. Toasting him is Julian Avery, Secretary of State for Air. Those present are believed to be (left to right): Lt-Col V. Konobeev Soviet Assistant Air Attaché (partially obscured behind Avery), Air Chief Marshal Sir Thomas Pike, Chief of the Air Staff, Unknown, Major-Gen I. P. Efimov, the Soviet Military Attaché and Ambassador Alexander Soldatov. *(RAF-T 2710)*

Taken by an unknown photographer, Vulcan B.2 XH561 of 50 Squadron, RAF Cottesmore, leads in 'Vic' formation four Lightning F.6s, XS922, XS894, XS903 and XR726 of 5 Squadron, RAF Binbrook, during a flight of April 1968, to mark the disbanding of Fighter and Bomber Commands and the formation of Strike Command. Little is known about the photographers who created most of these images. One, however, Malcolm (Mike) Chase was a Fellow of the Royal Photographic Society and an experienced photographer of aircraft in flight. He worked closely with pilots to achieve some of the spectacular air-to-air images in this collection. Flying in twin-seat training aircraft, he requested the pilots of the aircraft assume a range of flying attitudes to create the best images. *(RAF-T 8095)*

Five Harrier GR.1s of 1 Squadron are seen in starboard echelon formation during a training flight over Cyprus, July 1970. Images recording the introduction of new aircraft provide a glimpse of the RAF after 1970. In July 1969, 1 Squadron based at RAF Wittering reequipped with the Harrier. On 1 January 1970, it became the world's first operational squadron to fly a vertical/short take-off and landing (V/STOL) aircraft. The Harrier replaced the last remaining Hunter FGA.9s operating in the ground attack role. In the early images from the series, the introduction to service of the Hunter had itself been subject to proud RAF promotion. The Harrier was in service until 2010. *(RAF-T 5693)*

Chapter One

On the Front Line

After the Second World War, relations between the West and the Soviet Union deteriorated and the former wartime allies became adversaries. The blockade of Berlin from June 1948 indicated the Soviet Union's bellicose intentions in Europe and the world seemingly faced the prospect of another conflict. In Britain, war weariness and an economy in near total collapse, led to rapid demobilization and a general decline in RAF strength after 1945 and by 1948, the RAF found its front-line squadrons ill equipped for the Cold War.

In August 1949, the Commander-in-Chief of Fighter Command, Air Marshal Sir Basil Embry, began to strengthen Britain's air defences. Outdated wartime aircraft were struck off and by 1952, all front-line air defence squadrons were equipped with jet aircraft, the Gloster Meteor and de Havilland Vampire and Venom. Obsolete in comparison to the Soviet MiG-15, the Meteor was replaced as principal day fighter by the vastly superior Hawker Hunter. Introduced to service with 43 Squadron at RAF Leuchars in July 1954, the Hunter was serving in eighteen squadrons by 1959. The Gloster Javelin took up the night fighter role in August 1956 and together with the Hunter, provided Fighter Command's airborne defence for the rest of the decade. By 1964, both aircraft had been superseded by the supersonic English Electric Lightning, which entered service with 74 Squadron at RAF Coltishall in 1960, equipping all UK air defence squadrons until 1969 and the arrival of the Phantom.

In Germany at the start of the 1950s, the Second Tactical Air Force (2TAF) operated only thirteen Vampire day and three Meteor night fighter squadrons. Previously considered part of an occupation force, in 1951 2TAF's squadrons were assigned to NATO's Supreme Allied Commander Europe (SACEUR), becoming an integral part of European air defences within NATO's order of battle. The Command expanded to a peak of thirty-five squadrons by 1955, including ten squadrons of Canadair Sabre F.4s. In the following year, thirteen squadrons re-equipped with the Hunter, followed in August 1957 by the first Javelins, which entered service with 87 Squadron at RAF Brüggen. In 1965, the Lightning came to Germany, equipping 19 and 92 Squadrons.

The catastrophic 1957 Defence White Paper outlined a defence policy that prioritized nuclear over conventional forces and envisioned a surface-to-air missile system to protect the bomber bases, supported by a minimal force of manned fighters. As a result, Fighter Command was drastically reduced. From a post-war peak in 1956 of 600 front-line aircraft in thirty-five squadrons, by April 1962 it had shrunk to a mere 140 aircraft shared between eleven squadrons. The Second Tactical Air Force was initially cut from a total of thirty-five squadrons to seventeen, and by 1963 there remained just two air defence squadrons in Germany. The effect of these cuts was dramatic with squadrons disbanding almost overnight. This reduction in capability, compounded by further cuts in subsequent years, had an effect on the morale of RAF personnel for the next twenty years.

By 1970, despite cuts in numbers of aircraft and squadrons, RAF personnel in Britain and Germany had for twenty years successfully maintained interceptors and strike aircraft on permanent standby, ready for orders that could have signalled the start of nuclear war.

Following the detonation of the first Soviet nuclear weapon in August 1949, the potential threat to British cities from each unidentified radar contact grew considerably. Early interception was crucial. British air defences were, for the first time since the war, brought to a state of heightened readiness. From July 1950, day and night fighter squadrons provided a minimum of two aircraft at two-minute cockpit readiness under plans called Operation *Fabulous*. Operational Readiness Platforms (ORPs) were built alongside the runway, with Telebrief communication lines installed enabling aircrew to receive the order to scramble directly from the Sector Controller. From the early 1950s, improvements in ground-controlled interception and early warning radar increased Fighter Controllers' speed and accuracy in directing pilots to the contact before it reached the coast.

Initially, the principal threat was from the antiquated Soviet Tu-4 Bull, a copy of the American B-29. With the development of a Soviet long-range bomber and reconnaissance force, by the early-1960s the threat was from the Tu-16 Badger, Tu-95 Bear and the M-4 Bison, far more capable aircraft, which frequently approached UK airspace to test RAF defences. Working with the NATO early warning chain in Norway and Europe enabled much earlier detection, enabling interceptions further out at sea, and essential when Soviet aircraft started to carry stand-off missiles. In 1961 with UK air defence increasingly integrated with NATO, Fighter Command and UK air defences were assigned to SACEUR.

Throughout the 1950s and 1960s, air defence squadrons continued to maintain aircraft on heightened readiness. By the mid-1960s and now known as Quick Reaction Alert (QRA), this was held at just two Lightning-equipped air stations, RAF Leuchars, and alternately either RAF Binbrook or RAF Wattisham. Lightnings initially on the ORP were held at ten minutes' readiness in a dedicated QRA shed near the runway, which also provided accommodation for air and ground crews.

Similarly, a small number of aircraft from 2TAF's and later RAF Germany's air defence squadrons maintained Battle Flight, operating as part of NATO in the defence of Western European airspace. Due to the proximity of Soviet forces, Battle Flight was kept at a higher state of readiness than Fighter Command, with aircraft at two-minute readiness on ORPs, or later five minutes within hangars.

Maintaining QRA was the responsibility of personnel from across the station, not just aircrew. Operations staff and Air Traffic Control ensured air defence operations took priority with a team of ground crew responsible for the maintenance of QRA aircraft and aiding the pilot to achieve a rapid scramble. For ground crew, QRA or Battle Flight often provided a break from day-to-day routine, with crews occupying themselves with secondary tasks or recreation activities, interrupted by periods supporting QRA.

In 1950, as Fighter Command heightened Britain's air defences, Bomber Command looked to develop its ability to fight the war over enemy territory. While the V-Force of strategic nuclear bombers was under development, the RAF improved its force of conventional bombers. In May 1951, the English Electric Canberra, the RAF's first twin-jet bomber, entered service with 101 Squadron at RAF Binbrook.

Designed to be a fast lightly armed tactical bomber within 2TAF, the versatile Canberra assumed the role of principal bomber within Bomber Command's main force, replacing the obsolete Lincolns and Washingtons still in service. Production was made a priority and in early 1955, there were thirty-five Canberra squadrons in the UK and Germany. As sufficient numbers of V-bombers became operational, the Canberra was gradually withdrawn from UK service. The last main force Canberra squadron, 35 Squadron, disbanded in September 1961.

Remaining in RAF service, the Canberra eventually deployed to Germany as intended. In August 1954, 149 Squadron's Canberra B.2s moved from RAF Cottesmore to Gütersloh. Three further squadrons formed alongside it later that year. Between 1957 and 1958, following a growth of Soviet forces in Eastern Europe, the B.2 squadrons were replaced by squadrons of multi-role Canberra B(I)6s and B(I)8s specializing in low-level interdiction and close air support, a substantially different role from that undertaken by Canberra crews in the UK. With the cancellation of their replacement, the TSR.2 in 1965, Canberra B(I)8s remained in service in Germany until the early 1970s.

In their primary wartime role, the B(I)8s were issued American Mark 7 free-fall nuclear bombs, bringing a low-altitude, tactical, nuclear-strike capability to British forces in Germany. In this role, by January 1960, all four squadrons were maintaining QRA on behalf of NATO, with one loaded aircraft (two from 1962) at fifteen minutes' readiness. Aircraft were held in a QRA shed within a compound guarded by a combination of RAF and USAF armed police. QRA duty aircrew spent twenty-fours in this compound, accompanied by a USAF Alert Duty Officer who controlled access to the weapon. Prior to their QRA duty, each crew rigorously studied its assigned targets and flight profiles to provide an immediate response to SACEUR's call for a nuclear strike.

Throughout the 1950s and 1960s, in addition to QRA, life in the RAF was marked by regular training exercises. Interceptor pilots honed their skills in various air-defence manoeuvres, flying in battle formation or low-level interception known as 'rat and terrier'. No-notice scramble exercises tested aircrew and ground crews' ability to respond. Annual large-scale NATO air defence exercises were held over the UK or the Continent, during which training was held in conjunction with Bomber and Coastal Command squadrons which, as part of their own training, acted as the enemy force. In addition to simulating bombing raids on UK cities and ranges, Canberra B(I)8 crews practised low-flying around Germany, ending at the Nordhorn bombing range and a practice of the Low Altitude Bombing System (LABS) method of dropping nuclear weapons. This manoeuvre, as well as live firing and bombing training in the interdictor role, was frequently undertaken at locations in Germany, the UK or the ranges in Libya and Cyprus. Long-distance navigation flights by individual aircraft to the Mediterranean or Middle East, known as Southern Rangers, were a welcome break from QRA and routine training.

By the mid-1960s, NATO wide TACEVALs (Tactical Evaluations) were regularly being held to test the alertness of NATO forces. All aspects of Canberra QRA and Battle Flight – aircrew, ground crew and station operations – were evaluated. At individual stations, smaller MINEVALs (Minimum Evaluation) and wider RAF MAXEVALs (Maximum Evaluation) were also held prior to prepare for TACEVALs, together ensuring units were ready for unexpected operations. Generally loathed by air force personnel, by the 1970s TACEVALs had become synonymous with RAF service, particular in Germany. By the end of the Cold War in 1990, RAF Germany's nuclear strike Canberras, later replaced by Bucaneers, Phantoms, Jaguars and Tornados, had been on QRA for thirty years, while Battle Flight had been maintained for over forty. Today, RAF interceptors still maintain QRA, watching, waiting and ready to intercept.

Vampire NF.10 WP252 of 25 Squadron, seen with its Goblin engine characteristically torching on starting up, at RAF West Malling, 2 February 1952. Despite being a popular aircraft, the Vampire was not comfortable to fly. Within the cramped cockpit the pilot and navigator / radar operator sat side by side, the discomfort relieved by the pilot being positioned just slightly forward. Equipping 25 Squadron from 1951, the Vampire NF.10, along with the Meteor NF.11, replaced the Mosquito NF.36 in the night fighter role until the arrival of the Javelin in 1956. The Vampire was soon considered inadequate and was withdrawn from 25 Squadron by March 1954, replaced by the superior Meteor NF.14, which it operated until disbanding at RAF Tangmere in June 1958. *(RAF-T 30)*

At RAF Odiham, Javelin FAW.1s of 46 Squadron are prepared for a daytime training flight, on 23 July 1956. Javelins of 46 Squadron comprised one of the night fighter units, which as part of Operation *Fabulous*, undertook 'Night Fab' duties at Odiham, or on detachment to another station. Javelins were held on cockpit readiness on the ORP from dusk to dawn, and during bad weather, resulting in twenty-four hour operations during winter months. The two-man crews passed the ninety minutes until relieved dozing, chatting or playing ad hoc games. With a ten-crew flight, each crew would usually undertake two duties a night. In August 1957, 46 Squadron passed its FAW.1s to 87 Squadron at RAF Brüggen, replaced by FAW.2s. The squadron continued to operate the Javelin until disbanded in 1961. *(RAF-T 302)*

Hunter F.4s of 74 Squadron are seen on the busy pan at RAF Horsham St Faith during Exercise Vigilant, on 25 May 1957. Note the aircraft's white tail markings adopted for this exercise. Vigilant was the main air defence exercise of 1957. From Horsham St Faith, 74 Squadron, along with Javelins of 23 Squadron with 141 Squadron deployed from RAF Coltishall and 46 Squadron from Odiham, were pitted against eight 'enemy' raids over three days. 'Enemy' forces consisted of Bomber Command Canberras and Valiants, along with aircraft of 2TAF, a multinational NATO air force and naval aircraft from the US Sixth Fleet, based in the Mediterranean. Exercises weren't without risk. On the first morning of the exercise, two Hunters and one Javelin were destroyed through accidents, although with no loss of life. *(RAF-T 209)*

Senior Aircraftwoman Una Taylor, a photographer with 74 Squadron, talks with a pilot during Exercise Vigilant, on 25 May 1957. From its creation in 1948, the Women's Royal Air Force was integrated in the work and operations of the RAF. After separate basic entry, women trained and worked alongside male counterparts. One distinction made between the two sexes was pay. In 1960, SACWs were paid between £5 1s 6d and £6 16s 6d per week dependent on length of service, compared with £5 18s 0d to £8 1s 0d paid to men in the same trade. Initially 80 per cent of trades were open to women, with the exception of aircrew, RAF Regiment and most technical trades. In 1959, the Air Quartermaster trade was opened to women. In 1962, this trade was re-classified as aircrew, providing the WRAF with its first female aircrew. *(RAF-T 208)*

Canberra B.6s, WH948, WH958 and WT210, of 12 Squadron based at RAF Binbrook are seen in flight in September 1958, the squadron's fox head emblem visible on the aircraft's tails. Formed at Binbrook in June 1952, 12 Squadron was the third Bomber Command squadron to be equipped with the Canberra B.2. In May 1955, the squadron reequipped with the more powerful longer-ranged B.6. In November 1956, the squadron flew from Malta on low-level bombing raids in support of operations during the Suez Crisis. Despite the Canberra having a long service life, all three aircraft pictured here had unfortunate ends: WH948 crashed near RAF Coltishall after an engine fire in August 1977, WH958 crashed following a bird strike at Hong Kong in 1964, while WT210 crashed in 1988 whilst in service with No 6 Squadron, Indian Air Force. *(RAF-T 716)*

Shackleton MR.3 XF707 of 206 Squadron flying over the north coast of Cornwall near its home station of RAF St Mawgan in 1964. In February 1951, Coastal Command's Operational Conversion Unit at RAF Kinloss received the RAF's first Shackleton MR.1 maritime reconnaissance aircraft. By 1954, with an increase in Soviet naval activity, Shackletons were serving with eight squadrons, undertaking anti-submarine patrols from airfields in Scotland, Cornwall and Northern Ireland covering the Atlantic approaches to Britain, and one in Gibraltar covering the entrance to the Mediterranean. In each operational area, one Shackleton was maintained at one-hour readiness in the search and rescue role. In this role, in December 1963, Shackletons of 224 Squadron at Gibraltar searched for survivors of the stricken ship TSMS *Lakonia*, locating and dropping survival gear. *(RAF-T 4755)*

At RAF St Mawgan in Cornwall in 1964, armourers under the supervision of Chief Technician Swan disarm Shackleton MR.3 WR978 of 206 Squadron, following an anti-submarine warfare training sortie, while the aircraft is de-fuelled. The armourers are working on eight and a half pound break up bombs used to simulate depth charge attacks on participating friendly submarines. Behind them are seven day-glo red and blue active and passive Mark 1C sonobuoys used to detect and monitor enemy submarines. Regular training over the Atlantic, lasting between five and twelve hours, would test Shackleton crews' navigation skills, rehearse search and rescue procedures, radar homing procedures, surveillance techniques and attacks against a simulated submarine target, such as radio buoys. *(RAF-T 4758)*

Technicians servicing No. 3 engine of Shackleton MR.3 XF702 of 206 Squadron during the aircraft's stop in early 1963 at RAF North Front, Gibraltar. In the background are MR.2s of the resident 224 Squadron. Gibraltar was a regular destination for Shackleton crews undertaking training, either navigational exercises or multinational exercises, such as the annual NATO Exercise *Dawn Breeze*. During the Shackleton's operational patrols, some of which could last up to eighteen hours, the ten-man crew was subjected to noise and vibration from its four Griffon engines. Though the MR.3 was a vast improvement on the earlier versions, with better soundproofing, a proper galley and accommodation, it was still not considered comfortable. This mutually experienced discomfort forged the men of the Shackleton force into a tight team. On 21 December 1967, whilst flying in fog from RAF Kinloss, XF702 crashed in the Cairngorms killing all thirteen people on board. *(RAF-T 3041)*

An RAF medical officer climbs aboard Whirlwind HAR.2 XJ728 of 'A' Flight, 22 Squadron, based at RAF St Mawgan, but temporarily deployed to RAF Valley for mountain rescue exercises in 1957. In 1955, Coastal Command's search and rescue capability was bolstered when 22 Squadron, equipped with eight Whirlwind helicopters, was established at RAF Thorney Island. The following year, four 22 Squadron flights were detached to various stations around the UK. 'A' Flight was based at St Mawgan, 'B' Flight at RAF Felixstowe, 'C' Flight at RAF Valley and 'D' Flight at Thorney Island. One helicopter at each of these stations was held at fifteen-minute readiness during daylight to respond to emergencies. From June 1956, 22 Squadron headquarters also moved to St Mawgan. XJ728 was struck off charge in January 1960 after it crashed off Padstow, Cornwall, following tail rotor failure during a flight from RAF Chivenor. (RAF-T 347)

A Firestreak air-to-air missile on a dolly being transported by armourers to waiting Javelin FAW.9 XH887 of 23 Squadron based at RAF Leuchars detached to the Fighter Command Missile Practice Camp at RAF Valley on 13 May 1963. A red plastic 'Noddy' cap protects the infra-red missile's sensitive nose cone. Before Firestreak's introduction in 1958, interceptors had to be within range and position of their target to use their Aden cannons. Firestreak could be used at a range of five miles and from a number of different attack angles. Consequently, new interception techniques were developed at the Central Fighter Establishment at RAF West Raynham. The Javelin FAW.7 was the first aircraft to be fitted with air-to-air missiles as standard, carrying four missiles on underwing pylons. Two Firestreaks could also be carried by the Lightning, mounted on the forward fuselage. It remained in service until 1988. (RAF-T 4036)

A Lightning F.1A of 111 Squadron, armed with Firestreak missiles, is seen under floodlight preparing for a night sortie at RAF Wattisham in the summer of 1965. Wattisham was an important Cold War air defence station having, between 1950 and 1970, been at times home to squadrons of Meteors, Hunters, Javelins and Lightnings. By 1965, Wattisham was one of two stations maintaining QRA (South), alternating with RAF Binbrook, intercepting unidentified aircraft approaching from the east. Lightnings were held at ten-minute readiness during the day (or two minutes if at cockpit readiness) and thirty minutes at night. The pilots waited nearby, usually in a crew room, just moments from their aircraft. No. 111 Squadron received its Lightnings in April 1961 and after a period of work up was declared operational in September, undertaking air defence duties soon after. The squadron remained at Wattisham until 1974. *(RAF-T 5800)*

English Electric Lightning F.6s of 11 Squadron, armed with Red Top missiles are seen in tight, line abreast formation in the summer of 1967. From 1967, 11 Squadron, along with 23 Squadron, maintained QRA (North) from RAF Leuchars. Northern QRA had the demanding responsibility of intercepting the increasing number of Soviet aircraft approaching UK via the Arctic Circle or Norway. When scrambled by a radar station's Master Controller, the Lightning was guided to the intercept where the pilot would conduct a VISIDENT (visual identification) of the intruder, photographing any technical changes on the aircraft and shadowing it before returning home. No 11 Squadron, until January 1966 equipped with the Javelin at Geilenkirchen, received the Lightning F.6 in April 1967 when it reformed at Leuchars. It remained there until 1972. The second aircraft is XS904, which served only with 11 Squadron, and is currently preserved by the Lightning Preservation Group at Bruntingthorpe. (RAF-T 7510)

Seen here within the Operations Room at 'Southern Radar' based at RAF Sopley in 1966, an RAF Fighter Controller uses a Type 64 Plan Position Indicator console to direct air traffic. Southern Radar was one of several Air Traffic Control Radar Units in Britain using military ground-based radars to provide Air Traffic Control services for air traffic flying outside the UK's airways. Duties of the controllers at Southern Radar included providing Traffic Control or Traffic Information Services for aircraft operating over the South-West of the UK. In addition, Fighter Controllers at Sopley provided Ground Controlled Intercept practice for fighter pilots undergoing training at 229 OCU at RAF Chivenor. The Type 80 radar used at Sopley was introduced in 1953 and, when used in conjunction with American FNP-6 height finding radar, could accurately detect aircraft at 200 miles away and at up to 40,000ft. *(RAF-T 6162)*

The pilot of Lightning F.6 XR761 of 5 Squadron from RAF Binbrook guides his aircraft's refuelling probe into the drogue released from a Mark 20 underwing refuelling pod of Victor K.1 XA928 of 57 Squadron based at RAF Marham, in 1966. Air-to-air refuelling was an important role of the V-Force, initially being undertaken by the Valiant. Following the Valiant's retirement, the tanker role was assumed by the Victor. The first converted Victor bomber/tankers were received by 55 Squadron at Marham in May 1965. The scrambling of tankers from Marham during a QRA interception enabled the short-range Lightnings to patrol further from base for longer. The fuel was transferred through a drogue deployed by hose drum units situated either under the wing or in the bomb bay, with the flow of fuel activated by the pressure of the probe. XA928 originally served with 10 Squadron before being converted into a tanker, serving with 57 Squadron from March 1966. *(RAF-T 6270)*

Crew of Javelin FAW.9 XH911 of 5 Squadron at RAF Geilenkirchen, Germany, in April 1963. Maintaining a heightened alert state was a major undertaking. John Farley, a Hunter pilot of 4 Squadron at RAF Jever during the late-1950s recalled: 'it was 21–22 days a month that you were on some sort of formal standby duty on your squadron. It wasn't always you on the Battle Flight aeroplanes, but there were duty people in the hangar, duty people in the Ops Room, we were at a very high and continuous state of readiness … it was how you lived.' With the departure of the last Hunters in 1962, RAF Germany's Battle Flight was provided by Javelins of 5 and 11 Squadrons at Geilenkirchen. In October 1965, 5 Squadron was replaced by the Lightning F.2s of 19 Squadron at Gütersloh. XH911 was destroyed by fire during start up in September 1965. (RAF-T 4063)

A Lightning F.2 of 19 Squadron based at RAF Leaconfield is seen demonstrating its impressive climb ability over the East Yorkshire countryside in September 1965. Later that month, 19 Squadron became the first Lightning squadron to be deployed to RAF Germany, replacing 5 Squadron, which had reformed in the UK, also with Lightnings at RAF Binbrook. The limited range of the Lightning required 19 Squadron to be stationed at RAF Gütersloh, which at that time was the closest RAF station to the Air Defence Identification Zone and the East German border. In December 1965, 92 Squadron joined 19 Squadron in Germany, when it deployed to Geilenkirchen. It moved forward to join 19 Squadron at Gütersloh in January 1968. These two squadrons maintained the Battle Flight until late 1976. *(RAF-T 5847)*

At RAF Brüggen in West Germany, cameras are prepared for Canberra PR.7 WT518 of 80 Squadron, prior to a photoreconnaissance sortie c. 1965. A modified version of the Canberra B.2, the PR.3 was produced to fulfil the need for a strategic reconnaissance aircraft to replace the Meteor FR.10s and Mosquito PR.34 still in service. From 1954 one squadron of Canberra PR.3s and three of PR.7s were stationed with 2TAF in Germany to operate in the medium-range reconnaissance role operating along the NATO front from Norway to the Mediterranean. Alongside the Canberras, tactical reconnaissance was provided by Swift FR.5s, later replaced by Hunter FR.10s. No. 80 Squadron formed at RAF Laarbruch in July 1955, moving to Brüggen in June 1957. It remained there until disbanding in September 1969. *(RAF-T 4506)*

Guided missile fitters checking the launcher of a Bloodhound Mark I of 62 (SAM) Squadron at RAF Woolfox Lodge, 5 July 1961. Bloodhound was the proposed surface-to-air missile system envisioned in the 1957 Defence White Paper to protect the V-Force. From 1958, Bloodhound was deployed to eight sites, each equipped with sixteen missiles. RAF Woolfox Lodge was close to both the Victor wing at RAF Cottesmore and the Thor missile base at North Luffenham. From 1963, Bloodhound Mark I batteries were transferred to RAF Germany with 25 (SAM) Squadron. Interestingly, with various markings obscured, this is the only censored photograph in the collection. *(RAF-T 2705)*

Telegraphists relaying messages in the Message Hall at the Central Signals Centre, 'COMMCEN Central', RAF Stanbridge, in 1962. In recognition of the growing importance of radio, radar and electronic warfare, 90 (Signals) Group became Signals Command in November 1958. 'COMMCEN Central' was responsible for the receiving and transmitting of signals to RAF stations overseas. Telegraphists relayed messages by receiving and feeding Murray teleprint coded tape into the transmitters within the Message Hall. Signals between the UK and RAF Germany would be carried by GPO landline, while those to overseas stations were by High Frequency radio link, transmitted directly from the forest of aerials on the site or relayed via an intermediary station such as RAF Nairobi, Gan or Ceylon. In the early 1960s, over 10,000 messages were sent every day. After just ten years, Signals Command again became 90 (Signals) Group when it was absorbed into Strike Command in November 1968. *(RAF-T 2508)*

A captain of the Luftwaffe walks away from 14 Squadron's Canberra B(I)8 WT346 on the pan in front of Hangar 8 during an AFCENT Tactical Weapons Meet at Wildenrath, June 1967. From 1962, AFCENT TWMs were held annually to test the capability of NATO air forces in Germany. These competitions would assess participating aircrews in categories including bombing accuracy, navigation and night flying. In June 1967, the sixth competition was held at RAF Wildenrath, home to 14 Squadron. Competing were NATO's Second Allied Tactical Air Force, comprising 14 Squadron's Canberra B(I)8s, with aircraft from the Dutch, Belgian and German air forces against Fourth Allied Tactical Air Force consisting of American, Canadian and German aircraft. During the 1967 meet, a 14 Squadron crew, Flight Lieutenants J. Vernon (Pilot) and W. Yates (Navigator), won the night flying element and took second place overall behind the winning Canadian crew. *(RAF-T 7312)*

Canberra B(I)8 XM264 of 14 Squadron, crewed by Squadron Leader E. A. Taylor (pilot) and Flying Officer J. Parker (navigator), is marshalled to a halt in front of the Air Movements Squadron building at RAF Wildenrath during an AFCENT Tactical Weapons Meeting, June 1967. In its interdictor / intruder role, the B(I)8 was armed with a removable gun pack of four 20mm Aden cannons in the bomb bay. A range of bombs and rockets mounted on underwing pylons (just visible) could be used when shallow / dive bombing. Previously equipped with Hunters, 14 Squadron, reformed with Canberras at Wildenwrath in December 1962. The squadron moved to Brüggen in 1970 where it continued to operate in the nuclear strike role with RAFG until 1994. *(RAF-T 7282)*

Seen in late July 1968, a factory fresh McDonnell Douglas Phantom FGR.2 XT891 undergoes pre-service modifications at No. 23 Maintenance Unit, following delivery to RAF Aldergrove earlier that month. All 116 RAF ground-attack Phantoms that entered RAF service were received at Aldergrove, where they passed through 23MU for modifications prior to service. Generally popular with pilots for its power and capability, the Phantom was loathed by ground crew because of its difficulty to maintain, especially after modifications were made to enable the use of Rolls-Royce Spey engines. XT891 was the first RAF Phantom to be delivered to Aldergrove, arriving on 20 July 1968. In late August 1968 it went to 228 OCU at RAF Coningsby, before serving with 56 Squadron. Suffering several mechanical incidents, including a ground level ejection and several fires, it was retired and is currently the gate guardian at RAF Coningsby. *(RAF-T 9192)*

Chapter Two

The Nuclear Deterrent

With the delivery of the first 'Blue Danube' atomic bombs to RAF Wittering in 1953, the RAF became the guardian of the British nuclear deterrent. For the next sixteen years, it held this role, one that was a defining feature of RAF operations through the late 1950s and 1960s. For the servicemen selected to be responsible for this duty, life was characterized by continuous training with the weapon, and the aircraft and missiles designed to carry it, preparing for a mission they hoped they would never have to complete. In 1969, with concerns about the vulnerability of air stations and aircraft, the RAF passed control of its strategic deterrent to the Royal Navy and its Polaris submarines.

The British Government's quest for its own nuclear weapon culminated in 1952 and Operation *Hurricane*, which ended with the detonation of a nuclear device on the frigate HMS *Plym* at the Montebello Islands off Australia. The product of the test was Blue Danube, a 10-kiloton fission bomb weighing over 10,000lb. In August 1953, the Bomber Command Armament School was established at Wittering to handle the 'special store' and to train air and ground crews in its loading, before the first of the new aircraft, the Valiant, arrived in squadron service in early 1955. The following year No. 1321 Flight was formed, also at RAF Wittering, to coordinate the inert and (later) live dropping trials of Blue Danube. On 11 October 1956, during Operation *Buffalo*, Valiants from 49 Squadron became the first British aircraft to drop a live atomic bomb, doing so at the Maralinga range in the Australian outback.

In production from 1959, Red Beard was in operational service by the early 1960s. This was an improved bomb and had a larger yield, but weighed under a quarter of the weight of Blue Danube. Between May 1957 and September 1958, Operation *Grapple* resulted in the successful detonation of a thermonuclear (hydrogen) bomb at Christmas Island. Britain had become the third nation, after the USA and the Soviet Union, to detonate a megaton weapon, equal to more than one million tonnes of TNT. The resulting Yellow Sun supplemented Red Beard, replacing the last of the first generation Blue Danube atomic bombs in RAF service, and remained the principal free-fall nuclear bomb for the remainder of the RAF's guardianship.

In 1945, the latest long-range bomber in service with the RAF was the Avro Lincoln medium bomber, an antiquated four piston-engine bomber directly descended from the Avro Lancaster. These were partially replaced in 1951 by eighty-eight Boeing Washingtons lent by the USA under the Mutual Defence Assistance Programme (MDAP). In January 1947 the Ministry of Supply, with the delivery of future nuclear weapons in mind, issued order Specification B.35/46 on behalf of the Air Staff seeking designs for aircraft capable of carrying a 10,000lb bomb at heights of above 50,000ft, for over 3,500 miles. The successful designs formed the RAF's iconic nuclear capable Medium Bomber Force. The aircraft, the Vickers Valiant, Avro Vulcan and Handley Page Victor, were more commonly known as the V-Force.

The Valiant entered service in January 1955 with 138 Squadron at RAF Gaydon in Warwickshire, shortly before the formation there of 232 OCU, established to train crews on the new aircraft. The Avro Vulcan entered service with 230 OCU at RAF Waddington in February 1957 with the first operational aircraft being delivered across the Waddington airfield to 83 Squadron in July that year. The last of the V-Force, the Victor arrived in November 1957 at 232 OCU, which by now had switched to the training of Victor crews, before the first operational Victor squadron was formed as 10 Squadron at RAF Cottesmore in April 1958.

The V-bombers were the pinnacle of British aeronautical design. However, with the aircraft's cabins filled with banks of electronic equipment, the aircraft were uncomfortable to fly, with cramped cockpits and navigators and air electronics officers working in the dark rear compartments. Crews would spend many hours training in this claustrophobic environment.

Initially protected by a high flight ceiling (above 55,000ft for the Vulcan) and a near supersonic speed, the crews of the V-Force was confident in their ability to deliver the bomb. By the early 1960s, however, the deployment of Soviet surface-to-air missiles (SAMs), and the downing of Gary Powers's U2 reconnaissance aircraft over the Soviet Union in May 1960, threatened this confidence. Introduced to 617 Squadron in autumn 1962, the Avro Blue Steel 'stand-off' weapon was a rocket-powered missile launched from Vulcans and Victors. These missiles, guided by an internal navigation system, could cruise at Mach 1.8 for up-to 150 miles to the target, enabling the aircraft to stay beyond the range of the early SAMs. However, further technical advances raised concerns about the limited range of Blue Steel and despite the proposed development of a Blue Steel Mark 2 with a range of 1,000 miles, the programme was abandoned. Blue Steel was in service until 1970. In April 1964 Bomber Command switched the V-Force from high to an ultra-low altitude attack, sometimes as low as 100ft, thus under SAM radar cover. The Valiant was unsuited to low level flying and following the discovery of a resultant metal fatigue in the wing in August 1964 the aircraft was permanently grounded in January 1965.

In 1957, the UK agreed to host a US-UK jointly operated missile: the Douglas Thor Intermediate Range Ballistic Missile. Incapable of striking the Soviet Union from America, the first of sixty Thor missiles were installed on stations along the east coast of England, becoming operational in August 1958. They were jointly manned by the RAF who had control of the sites and the launch of the missiles and the USAF 99th Support Squadron who controlled access to and the arming of the 1.4MT nuclear warhead.

Following the introduction in 1962 of Minuteman missiles capable of being launched from the United States along with the delivery of Blue Steel to squadrons, Thor, Britain's only surface-launched ballistic missile, was withdrawn by August 1963.

The launch of Sputnik by rocket in 1957 highlighted the potential vulnerability of V-Force bases and Thor sites from a decisive Soviet missile strike, a fact not lost on the men who worked at the RAF stations or their families, who lived in nearby accommodation. It was essential that the V-bombers were airborne quickly, initially within fifteen minutes. From February 1962, Bomber Command adopted the NATO Quick Reaction Alert (QRA) system across the V-Force, having at least one armed and fuelled aircraft from each squadron placed on dispersal, or on Operational Readiness Platforms at the end of the runways. For the crews on standby, there were invariably long periods of inactivity. Weekdays could be filled with planning training sorties or studying target information, but weekends without regular squadron activities were often dull, with little to do. QRA duty during the Christmas period was considered particularly tiresome.

For the men of the V-Force and Thor squadrons, life was marked by regular QRA and exercises. Punctuating the routine, Group HQ or Bomber Command called simulated scrambles where V-Force and missile crews had to prove their ability to launch in the required time. Well publicized and regular practice was essential to show readiness and capability, thus ensuring the success of the weapon as a deterrent.

By 1962, with the cancellation of the proposed US long-range Skybolt air-launched cruise missile project and the British Blue Streak MRBM, Britain was left without a future means of delivering its nuclear weapons. In August 1962, it was decided that Polaris, the American submarine-launched missile system, would be provided for use by Royal Navy submarines. In 1968, the first of these submarines, HMS *Resolution*, became operational. With the commissioning of the final Polaris submarine the following year, the RAF lost its guardianship of Britain's nuclear deterrent, though it retained tactical nuclear weapons until 1996.

The three V-bombers in flight together, 13 January 1958, soon after the introduction to service of the final aircraft, the Victor. The different design responses to the Air Staff's 1946 specification are clearly seen. The first Victor, XA931 of 232 OCU, is seen on the left led by Vulcan XA904 of 83 Squadron, with Valiant XD869 of 214 Squadron on the right. The conservatively designed Valiant was accepted as an insurance policy against delay or failure in the delivery of the revolutionary and complex Vulcan and Victor, the Air Ministry's two preferred aircraft. By the end of 1957, despite having nearly 100 Valiants in service, and with the supply of Vulcans well under way, the V-Force had a stockpile of only twenty Blue Danube atomic bombs. (RAF-T 531a)

Valiant B(K).1 XD829 of 49 Squadron seen during a flight from its base at RAF Wittering, September 1957. The Valiant was the first British aircraft to drop an atomic bomb, 49 Squadron's WL366 doing so during the Operation *Buffalo* trials in the Australian desert in October 1956. The following year, Valiant XD818 also of 49 Squadron dropped Britain's first hydrogen bomb during Operation *Grapple* in the Pacific. XD829 was one of the eight Valiants involved in Operation *Grapple*. To protect these aircraft from the effects of heat from a thermonuclear explosion, the participating Valiants were painted in the now familiar 'anti-flash white' paint scheme. This scheme was later introduced across the Valiant and Vulcan fleets and to the Victor as it entered service. *(RAF-T 219)*

Vulcan B.1 XA906 of 83 Squadron is seen under tow by a Douglas Sentinal Tugmaster heavy towing unit at RAF Waddington c. October 1957, a few months after the Vulcan entered service. Vulcan B.1 XA906 was the third aircraft to be delivered to a front-line squadron, arriving with 83 Squadron at RAF Waddington on 12 August 1957. It was converted to B.1A standard in March 1962, re-entering service with 44 Squadron in August 1962. With the introduction of Vulcan B.2, XA906 went into storage at RAF St Athan in 1967 and was scrapped in November 1968. The Tugmaster was introduced in the mid-1950s to tow the heavy aircraft that entered service during the period, including the V-bombers and the Comet. *(RAF-T 339)*

Squadron Leader Ulf L. Burberry and his crew race towards Victor B.1 XH592 of XV Squadron, during a demonstration scramble at RAF Cottesmore, in June 1959. The crew chief is ready on the intercom to the cockpit while a member of ground crew removes the chocks. The Victor was the last and the longest serving of the V-bombers, seeing service between November 1957 and 1993. In addition to its nuclear and conventional bomber role, following the retirement of the Valiant in the mid-1960s, the Victor assumed the roles of principal refuelling tanker and strategic reconnaissance aircraft. By 1969, and the loss of the strategic role to the Royal Navy all remaining Victors were converted into tankers. Having served only with XV Squadron, in June 1965 XH592 was transferred to the Tanker Training Flight at RAF Marham. *(RAF-T 1018)*

Flight Lieutenant S. Price and his crew in front of a Valiant B(PR)K.1, probably of 138 Squadron at RAF Wittering, October 1957. Each type of V-bomber carried a crew of five: a captain, co-pilot, navigator-radar (bomb-aimer), navigator-plotter and air electronics officer (initially called signallers). V-Force aircrew were selected based on experience; nobody could volunteer. Pilots required an accumulated 1,750 hours flying as first pilot as well as experience on jets and four-engine aircraft; co-pilots needed 700 hours' flying. Navigator-radars had to have completed at least one tour on Canberras. Many of the early crews were experienced wartime aircrew of high rank, reinforcing the perception that the V-Force was an elite unit. On the early Valiants, a limited number of trained officer navigators and signallers necessitated the recruitment of highly experienced senior NCOs. However, only officers could be in a position of responsibility for the nuclear weapon. *(RAF-T 312)*

The captain of a Victor B.1, probably of XV Squadron, based at RAF Cottesmore, is seen seated in his left-hand position as if in flight, in April 1959. The Air Ministry praised the Victor for its 'excellent vision and roomy comfort of the cockpit' while *Flight* Magazine in 1957 described the equipment as 'producing an atmosphere at once spacious and intimate'. Of the three V-bombers, the Victor was considered by pilots as the most comfortable to fly with the Valiant and the Vulcan having significantly smaller cockpits. The navigators and the AEO were positioned in a row behind the cockpit facing the rear, separated by a black-out curtain. Note the ejector seat. In all three V-bombers, only the pilot and co-pilot were able to have ejector seats. The other three crew members would bale out through the fuselage door. *(RAF-T 1060)*

The navigator-radar's position in the rear crew section of an unidentified Vulcan B.2, c. 1965. He is watching the green screen of the H2S radar during a simulated bombing run. He would adjust the direction of the radar to fix on the target by using the joystick in his right hand. The navigator-radar would use the H2S radar and the Navigation and Bombing Computer to direct the aircraft manually, or by autopilot, and arm the weapon as they approached the target. In an August 1966 interview with the *Sunday Telegraph*, Flight Lieutenant Mike Rollins, navigator-radar of a Vulcan squadron of the Waddington Wing, expressed the feelings of many V-Force rear crew: '*in Fighter Command you were free, you could see out of the plane. Flying Vulcans is more relaxed but you're completely enclosed with four other men in a small black hole completely surrounded by thousands of instruments.*' (RAF-T 4153)

The navigator-plotter of Victor B.1 XH928 of 10 Squadron at RAF Cottesmore, seen in position through the window of the visual bomb aiming position, June 1959. Each of the three V-bombers had a visual bombing position that gave the bomb aimer an optically flat view of the ground below. This allowed, in clear weather, more accurate visual targeting, even at altitudes of over 50,000ft. As the navigator-radar guided the aircraft to the target, the navigator-plotter would squeeze into and lay in the cramped position, sometimes for extended periods at a time, to visually confirm the target and using the bombsight provided allow the release of the payload. (RAF-T 1010)

Vulcan B.1 XA904 of 83 Squadron is raised off the ground by cradles and jacks while undergoing servicing at RAF Waddington, October 1957. The design of the Vulcan allowed most servicing to be undertaken from under the aircraft. Maintenance was crucial to the effectiveness of the V-Force. Responsibility for each aircraft was given to an experienced crew chief, usually a chief technician, leading a skilled ground crew of advanced tradesmen from a range of different trades. Before each aircraft type arrived in service, the manufacturers provided intensive courses to prepare first generation ground crew for working on the new aircraft. XA904 was the second aircraft delivered to a front-line squadron, arriving at 83 Squadron on 16 July 1957. It was converted to B.1A standard in January 1961, re-entering service with 44 Squadron. On 28 February 1961 it crashed at Waddington having run out of fuel while landing and was struck off charge. (RAF-T 416)

The aircrew of a Victor B.1 of 57 Squadron, based at RAF Honington, go through external pre-flight checks at RAF Cottesmore, July 1959. The crew chief often travelled as the sixth crew member when an aircraft spent time away from its home station. However, aircrew were required to know how to 'turn-around' the aircraft without assistance. In cases of enforced landing, they were able to refuel, repair and prepare for take-off, without risking the aircraft's security by exposing it to an inexperienced ground crew. *(RAF-T 1069)*

An unidentified Valiant B(K).1 of 49 Squadron of the Tactical Bomber Force being defuelled following a sortie at RAF Marham in April 1964. With the Vulcan and Victor force force at near full strength by July 1961, the three Marham-based Valiant squadrons, 207, 49 and 148, were assigned to NATO under the command of Supreme Allied Commander Europe for use in the tactical bombing role using American Mark 28 nuclear weapons. SACEUR required one aircraft and crew from each of the squadrons be maintained at 15-minute readiness, the first time QRA was applied to the V-Force. The aircraft is painted in dark green and medium grey tactical camouflage reflecting the change from the high to low-level flying adopted in early 1964. Note: the retention of the anti-flash white underside can just be seen under the open crew hatch. (RAF-T 4885)

Vulcan B.2s of 83 Squadron, based at RAF Waddington, on the ORP at RAF Finningley during a dispersal exercise, late 1961. Readiness State 15 (RS15), i.e. fifteen minutes to launch, could be held for four weeks. Flight Lieutenant Rollins describes QRA: '*The worst QRA duties are at weekends when you can't plan sorties at the squadron. You have to rely on amusements. You get a bit sick of table tennis and mooch around looking for something to do.*' Crews would either alternate QRAs every 24 hours or take a shift lasting several days. Readiness states of RS05 with crews seated in the aircraft, or RS02 with engines started were possible. During the Cuban Missile Crisis of October 1962, the entire V-Force was at a heightened readiness state with crews sat in their aircraft. *(RAF-T 2843)*

Three Vulcan B.2s of 617 Squadron, carrying Blue Steel training rounds, demonstrate a dispersal scramble at RAF Scampton on 9 August 1963. From the late 1950s, to protect the V-Force from a pre-emptive strike, aircraft could be dispersed to twenty-six airfields across the UK. In addition to twice monthly exercises to test QRA readiness, Exercise Mickey Finn was held at least once a year, when all aircraft at a station, and occasionally the entire V-Force, were dispersed simultaneously. These exercises often ended in simulated bombing exercises over British cities. In the film *Delta 8-3* (1960), which follows a Waddington crew, the narrator states: '*The job isn't really to drop bombs on people; it's not to drop bombs. To keep fit and efficient, to practise flying Vulcans to specified places at specified times. If the day ever comes when the bombs are real and the target hostile, it will all have been in vain.*' (RAF-T 4133)

Armourers load a dummy Yellow Sun Mark 2 into the capacious bomb bay of a Victor B.1A, during Exercise Unison at RAF Honington, 1963. The Yellow Sun Mark 2 thermonuclear weapon had an estimated yield of 1.2 megatons and was the single most potent weapon in the RAF's arsenal. Issued to the V-Force from 1960, Yellow Sun replaced Blue Danube as the payload for the Vulcan B.1As and Victor B.1As. The complicated and time-consuming process of loading the 7,000lb weapon illustrated the need for keeping aircraft ready armed and on QRA. As well as loading exercises, armourers would replace an operational bomb with a dummy during dispersal exercises. *(RAF-T 4141)*

Vulcan B.2 XM599 of 35 Squadron based at RAF Cottesmore releases a full bomb load of twenty-one 1000lb bombs, during an exercise, in 1965. As well as operating in the nuclear role each of the V-bombers had the capability to deliver conventional ordnance. The Valiant and the Vulcan were both able to carry twenty-one 1,000lb bombs, while the Victor carried thirty. Approximately twice a year each V-Force crew would undertake live bombing exercises. These short overseas deployments were eagerly sought by crews to break the monotony of QRA training and exercises. Each type of bomber was used in action only once. The Valiant was the first to see action during the 1956 Suez campaign, followed by a single raid by two Victors during the Indonesian Confrontation and the Vulcan Black Buck raids during the Falklands Conflict. (RAF-T 5756)

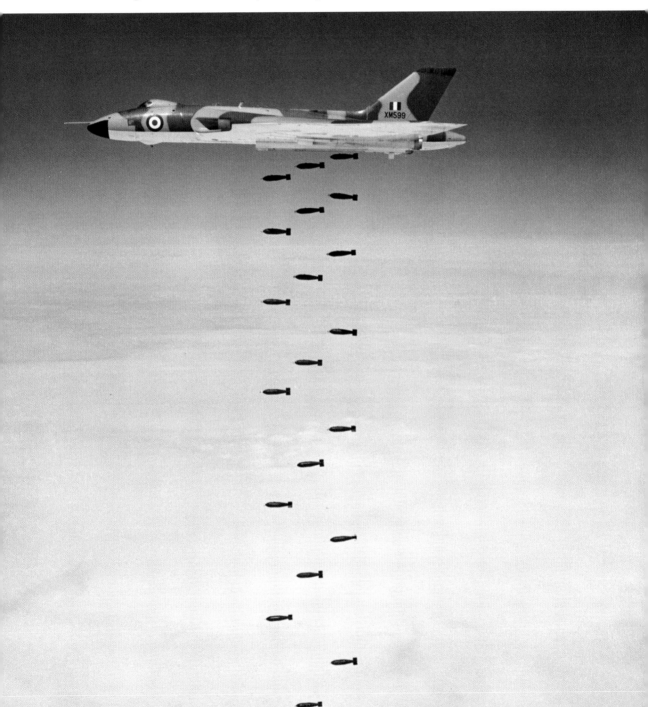

Floodlights add to the menacing sight of a Thor countdown exercise at night by 77 (SM) Squadron at RAF Feltwell in November 1958. The tank in the foreground holds kerosene, part of the missile's propellant. Each 90ft missile sat on an erector, which doubled as a transporter. Its wheels are visible at the base of the missile. The sixty Thor missiles were based at four complexes, each consisting of a main base and four satellite stations, each with three launch pads and manned by a missile squadron. The main bases were at RAF stations Feltwell, North Luffenham, Driffield and Helmswell. Thor was completely different to anything else in the RAF inventory. Len Townend, a missile maintenance technician of 107 (SM) Squadron at RAF Tuddenham was impressed: '… *no doubt about it, they were a marvellous weapon … we had Bloodhound [surface to air] missiles but Thors were far in advance of anything we had.' (RAF-T 876)*

Three senior NCO missile maintenance technicians check the internal systems of a Thor missile of 77 (SM) Squadron at RAF Feltwell in November 1958. Day-to-day the missiles were stored horizontally on their erector within a retractable weather-proof shelter in a semi-dormant, 'standby' state. MMTs conducted frequent missile checks to ensure they retained operational status. Each missile squadron had a commanding officer, five launch control officers, five further aircrew and fifty-nine ground crew, which included the MMTs. Approximately 1,200 Bomber Command personnel served directly on Thor during its time in service, with another 3,000 in support working as administrative or training staff. Squadron personnel stationed on the main bases enjoyed the varied facilities usually found at operational RAF stations. At the smaller and remote satellite stations, often hurriedly converted from old wartime sites, personnel found limited accommodation or recreational facilities available to them. *(RAF-T 881)*

Liquid oxygen, part of the fuel for a Thor missile, boils off under pressure during a 'wet countdown' by an unidentified Thor missile squadron, c. 1961. At least one missile from each squadron was kept at a state of fifteen minutes from launch (T-15). Missiles could also be brought to T-8 briefly with the missile raised, or T-2 fuelled with kerosene and liquid oxygen (LOX). Twice a month, a 'dry countdown' was held, raising the missile and checking electrical systems. During an infrequent 'wet countdown', the missile was filled with LOX. HQ Bomber Command's order to initiate the launch sequence was received in the launch control centre, often a caravan near the launch pad. The American authentication officer received his order to arm the warhead from Strategic Air Command in Nebraska. On 27 October 1962, during the Cuban Missile Crisis, fifty-nine of the sixty Thor missiles were brought to readiness T-15. *(RAF-T 2612)*

V-Force bases and Thor missile sites were regularly targeted by protest groups including the fledgling Campaign for Nuclear Disarmament. Guarding against unauthorized access was the responsibility of the RAF Police or, if using American weapons, the USAF Police. Each Thor site was allocated an RAF police sergeant and twelve corporals, with a dog handler supplied at night or times of high activity. Len Townend at RAF Tuddenham: 'We used to get ban the bomb people come down and have a go at you. They used to come around at the weekends and shout at the gates and that, and try to climb over the wire … We never had any real trouble from them, but they had to be repelled.' Despite the regular testing of security by enthusiastic 'undercover' airmen of the RAF Regiment, the on-site American personnel and visiting dignitaries thought British security was woefully inadequate. (RAF-T 4053)

In 1963, RAF Fylingdales with its distinctive 'golf ball' radar domes, was constructed on the North Yorkshire moors as part of a chain of American-built radar stations, the others being at Thule, Greenland and in Clear, Alaska. These stations tracked objects in low orbit around the earth, monitoring potential missile launches and predicting targets. Data picked up at Fylingdales would be assessed and credible threats would be passed to HQ Bomber Command at RAF High Wycombe. If confirmed, the Royal Observer Corps and the UK Monitoring and Warning Organization (UKMWO) would alert the population to take preparatory measures. The notice period between detection of an incoming missile and impact was said to be four minutes. In reality it would have been considerably less. *(RAF-T 4180)*

Air Chief Marshal Sir Wallace Kyle, AOC-in-C Bomber Command (right), observes a test of the Ballistic Missile Early Warning System in August 1965 with AOC No. 1 Group Air Vice-Marshal Stapleton and the CO of RAF High Wycombe. Information received by the BMEWS at RAF Fylingdales would be relayed to HQ Bomber Command at High Wycombe. The AOC Bomber Command would monitor the situation assessing the threat and alert the V-Force. On instruction from the Prime Minister he would instigate a scramble. *(RAF-T 5979)*

Vulcan B.2 XL317 of 617 Squadron based at RAF Scampton carries a Blue Steel practice round during a flight in February 1963. Blue Steel was introduced to squadron service in August 1962. Blue Steel was designed to be launched over 100 miles from target, beyond the range of Soviet SAMs. Under Blue Steel's initial flight profile. It would have been released at a height of approximately 50,000ft, from which it would free fall to 30,000ft, the engine would ignite and propel it at over twice the speed of sound to a height of 70,000ft before cutting off, allowing it to glide to its target. Twenty-six Vulcan B.2s were modified to carry Blue Steel; all served with the Scampton Wing. *(RAF-T 3584)*

Technicians work on the Stentor engine of a Blue Steel missile in the Missile Servicing and Storage Building (MSSB) at RAF Scampton in February 1963. Despite its size, Blue Steel was a delicate weapon. Its inertia guidance system was very sensitive, its electrics reacted to extremes of temperature and it was powered by High Test Peroxide, a very volatile fuel of a mixture of hydrogen peroxide and kerosene. Generally unpopular with armourers, Blue Steel required regular maintenance and very careful handling, making it difficult to fuel, transport and load. *(RAF-T 3584)*

At RAF Wittering, armourers use an AEC Matador airfield munitions truck to lower a Blue Steel onto a dolly for transportation to a waiting Victor B.2, 1964. The aircraft is painted dark green and medium grey, following the change to low altitude flying. Introduced to handle Blue Steel, this version of the Matador contained equipment to monitor the state of the volatile fuel during its journey to the aircraft. Once there the missile was transferred to a dolly and positioned under the aircraft. Loading the missile proved problematic, not least because of the difference in ground clearance between the Vulcan bomb bay and that of the Victor. The total clearance when loading a Blue Steel in a Victor was just fourteen inches. *(RAF-T 4862)*

A Blue Steel is carefully positioned under the specially modified bomb bay of Vulcan B.2 XL318 of 617 Squadron at RAF Scampton in February 1963. Note the aircraft is painted with Type D pale roundels introduced as part of the protection against the heat of a thermonuclear blast. In February 1963, 617 Squadron was declared at operational strength with Blue Steel, followed by 27 and 83 Squadrons to complete the reequipping of the Scampton Wing. By early 1964, the Victors of 100 and 139 Squadrons at RAF Wittering were also operational. The requirement to have fully armed and fuelled Blue Steel in aircraft on QRA initially caused concerns within Bomber Command. After realizing that it took upwards of an hour for the weapon to be prepared, the Air Ministry cleared Blue Steel to be mated to aircraft on QRA in August 1964. *(RAF-T 3619)*

Vulcan B.1 XA912 of 101 Squadron based at RAF Finningley, flies over Mount Kenya during a 'Lone Ranger' flight to Nairobi in July 1960. An established part of the training for V-Force aircrew and crew chiefs, Lone Rangers were unsupported single aircraft detachments to destinations around the world, including Cyprus, Malta, Singapore and Australia. These were exercises in self-sufficiency as servicing facilities were usually not available and all maintenance was undertaken by the crew. Lone Rangers provided experience in operating in varied climatic conditions and terrain. Variations on the Lone Ranger included Southern Ranger, which extended as far south as Kenya and Rhodesia, and Western Ranger to bases in Canada and the US. These annual overseas detachments were eagerly sought by crews as they provided a relief from day-to-day operational training and QRA. *(RAF-T 1965)*

Chapter Three

The RAF Overseas

Recruitment brochures promoted a career in the RAF as a route to foreign travel, and until the late 1960s, opportunity was certainly plentiful and varied. A large amount of manpower was needed to service the strategic stations in the Middle East and Far East, along with the more isolated stations elsewhere. For many personnel, an overseas tour was a highlight of their career, yet by 1971 a posting of significant length was rare. Decolonization and budgetary pressures led Britain (and the RAF) to rapidly withdraw from its responsibilities overseas, first in the Middle East, then the Far East. This withdrawal was often complicated by the many small-scale yet intensive conflicts that occurred during the period.

There were few times between 1950 and 1970 when the RAF was not actively involved in a conflict somewhere in the world.

Operations during the twelve-year Malayan Emergency were largely shaped by the need to cooperate with ground units operating in inaccessible jungle. From 1948, troops on patrol were supported by low-flying ground attack aircraft such as the Brigand and later the Hornet, Vampire and Venom, targeting enemy camps and supply lines. In the early part of the Emergency, under Operations *Musgrave* and *Bold*, Lincoln bombers from six UK-based squadrons were deployed in rotation to RAF Tengah in Singapore to boost the RAF's offensive power. In February 1955, the Lincolns were replaced in the Far East by Canberras. Deep jungle patrols were aided with air resupply by Douglas Dakotas, Vickers Valettas and Handley Page Hastings of 48 Squadron, and later by Scottish Aviation Pioneer and Auster light aircraft of 267 and 209 Squadrons. Support was also provided by Dragonfly and Sycamore helicopters of 194 Squadron, joined later by Westland Whirlwinds of 110 and 155 Squadrons. Over an eighteen-month period during 1954–55, 194 Squadron alone flew 6,000 sorties, transporting 84,000lb of supplies and evacuating 675 casualties from remote jungle locations.

During the summer of 1956, while the RAF was busy in South East Asia, Colonel Nasser nationalized the Suez Canal. The RAF reinforced its Middle East Air Force squadrons and assembled a formidable force in Cyprus and Malta, including 115 Valiant and Canberra bombers, forty-eight Venom fighter-bombers and twenty-four Hunters. For the Anglo-French Suez operation, the RAF was tasked with destroying Egypt's Air Force of Il-28 bombers, MiG-15s, Vampires and Meteors, which posed a threat to the invasion force assembled in Cyprus. Four squadrons of Valiants, along with squadrons of Canberras, undertook high and low-altitude bombing of Egyptian airfields and military installations, accompanied by rocket and cannon-armed Venoms from 6, 8 and 249 Squadrons. Providing transport for the airborne invasion, Valetta and Hastings flew 3rd Battalion Parachute Regiment from Cyprus escorted by Hunters of 1 and 34 Squadrons, deployed from RAF Tangmere. Adding to the complexity of the operation, local air forces in Cyprus were combating the four-year EOKA insurgency.

From 1963, the RAF used the experience it had gained during the Malayan Emergency in an undeclared jungle war with Indonesia on the Island of Borneo. Ground forces operating from forward bases in remote parts of the island relied entirely on air power for reinforcement and resupply. Two Blackburn Beverleys from 34 Squadron and two Armstrong Whitworth Argosys from 215 Squadron from Singapore were detached to Labuan and Kuching to resupply troops via drop zones in the jungle. Pioneers and Twin Pioneers of 209 Squadron provided a light supply, troop lifts and casualty evacuation capability from forward airstrips, aided by Bristol Belvederes of 26 Squadron and by Whirlwinds of 103, 110, 225 and 230 Squadrons, which most notably inserted troops over the Indonesian border on secretive *Claret* operations. Between November 1964 and October 1965, the monthly average weight of stores delivered to front-line bases was nearly 3,000,000lb. In addition Javelins of 60 and 64 Squadrons and Hunters of 20 Squadron from Tengah, Labuan and Kuching undertook air defence patrols following an increasing number of incursions by the Indonesian Air Force. Canberras from Bomber Command and the Akrotiri Strike Wing deployed to the region on rotation, reinforced by Victors and Vulcans.

By early 1964, having been strengthened to combat two successive rebellions in the Radfan region of South Arabia, RAF Khormaksar's Tactical Wing was a formidable force, with a combined forty-eight Hunter FGA.9s from 8, 43 and 208 Squadrons and four Hunter FR.10s from 1417 Flight. During the campaigns, the RAF provided tactical support to British troops engaging rebel tribesmen in the mountainous terrain. Rocket-carrying Hunters carried out air strikes against targets identified from photographs provided by 1417 Flight. Shackleton MR.2s of 37 Squadron flew night-time bombing raids, dropping 25lb fragmentation bombs and illumination flares. Twin Pioneers of 78 Squadron and Beverleys of 84 Squadron moved men and materiel to upcountry airstrips at Thumeir and Dhala, where Belvederes of 26 Squadron ferried them further forward.

Following the end of British Government in Aden in 1967, Air Support Command mounted a three-month airlift of 6,600 civilians to RAF Muharraq in Bahrain, followed by the last 3,700 servicemen using Short Belfasts, Bristol Britannias and the new Lockheed Hercules.

The RAF's operational role in all these conflicts was providing flexible tactical air support for troops fighting over inhospitable terrain. This differed from the traditional role of air superiority and heavy bombing that had been its dominant contribution during the Second World War. Instead, it returned to a role it had been founded to undertake in 1918. The RAF was also employed on numerous humanitarian missions during the British Honduras hurricane in 1961, famine in East Africa in 1962 and floods in Brunei in 1963.

The RAF's Cold War responsibilities did not exist solely within Europe. A member of NATO since 1948, Britain was also a signatory of the 1954 South East Asia Treaty Organization (SEATO) and the 1955 Baghdad Pact, later called the Central Treaty Organization (CENTO). Though no military assets were permanently assigned to SEATO, squadrons and airfields of the Far East Air Force and the regular V-bombers detached to the region could be requested by SEATO, and regularly participated in frequent exercises with other regional powers. In 1957, a Near East Strike Wing of Canberra bombers from 6, 32, 73 and 249 Squadrons was formed at RAF Akrotiri in Cyprus. This wing was assigned to CENTO, whose member states Turkey, Pakistan, Iran, and originally Iraq, extended NATO's reach east along the southern border of the USSR yet lacked a bombing capability of their own. In 1969,

Canberras were replaced in the strike wing by two squadrons of Vulcans from RAF Cottesmore with two further squadrons held in reserve in the UK. By the late 1960s, active support of these alliances diminished when long-distance transports and in-flight refuelling capabilities allowed UK-based units to deploy rapidly, reaching Cyprus within a few hours and Singapore within a couple of days.

The large number of stations and units based overseas ensured that, for the majority of personnel in the 1950s and 1960s, at least one tour could be expected. The RAF's commitments from the late 1940s combined with the demobilization of a large number of regular personnel ensured that fulfilling all overseas obligations, one in two, though later decreased to less than one in four, of RAF National Servicemen were out of the UK for most of their two-year service.

As the RAF withdrew from its worldwide commitments, overseas service became increasingly rare. The movement towards decolonization in the early to mid-1950s saw the, often forced, withdrawal from a large number of RAF stations. Rising Arab nationalism in the mid-late 1950s saw the RAF leave the Middle East. Between 1956 and 1959 the RAF handed over its last stations in the Suez Canal Zone, Jordan and Iraq, all key staging posts on the route east to Singapore. The remnants of the Middle East Air Force stationed at these locations were withdrawn and relocated to RAF Nicosia in Cyprus. Already considerably smaller in 1950 than it had been in 1945, the Far East Air Force shrunk further in the late 1950s, when further staging posts RAF Mauripur in Pakistan closed in 1957 and RAF Negombo in Ceylon in 1959. During its Emergency, Malaya had been given its independence in 1957, and the last RAF units were withdrawn to Singapore in 1960, which became the centre for British forces in the Far East.

The economic conditions of the mid-1960s, combined with further nationalist unrest, saw the end to further historic stations. RAF Nicosia in Cyprus, once the principal air base in the Near East, was closed in 1966 in favour of the newer RAF Akrotiri. After the hurried evacuation of Aden in 1967, RAF Muharraq in Bahrain was the last remaining station in the Persian Gulf. The Libyan revolution in 1969 saw the RAF forced to leave RAF El Adem, its last station in North Africa. The 1968 Defence Review announced that all RAF stations 'East of Suez' with the exception of Hong Kong were to close by 1971. In that year, the Far East Air Force was disbanded and its principal stations of Changi, Tengah, and Seletar were handed to Singapore. With forces still based in Cyprus, Malta and Hong Kong, opportunities for overseas service still existed, but the accompanied postings to Singapore, Cyprus or Aden, which had for fifty years often been the highlight of an RAF career, were no longer available.

In March 1957, two Valiant B.1s from 207 Squadron (one seen here) and two from 148 Squadron, travelled from their base at RAF Marham to Accra in the Gold Coast (Ghana) to represent Great Britain at celebrations to mark the country's independence. Accompanying them were two Comets from 216 Squadron carrying the Valiants' ground crews, some of whom are seen talking to soldiers of the Gold Coast Regiment. In addition to full length tours of up to two and a half years, personnel were deployed for shorter periods on a range of duties or exercises. Most commonly individual aircraft or at flight or squadron strength, were detached to supplement regional forces during emergencies. Participation in navigation exercises or bombing exercises allowed crews short periods away from their day-to-day duties. *(RAF-T 375)*

Three officers, who accompanied Secretary of State for Air George Ward during a tour of South America, relax in Rio de Janeiro, April 1958. Ward travelled in a Comet of 216 Squadron, escorted by Vulcans of 83 Squadron, promoting the latest aircraft in RAF service. For men who joined the RAF to travel, detachments to remote countries to 'fly the flag' or postings to work alongside NATO allies provided the opportunity to visit places that were not the usual deployment locations. In 1961, Pilot Officer Peter Symes as the Junior Accountant Officer at Marham was summoned to the Squadron Commander: *'he informed me that my name had come up for a short notice requirement [at USAFB Hickam] in Hawaii. If I accepted, I would need to be there in a month's time, so he would let me think about it. I immediately said that I had!' (RAF-T 603)*

Four Vampire FB.9s of 213 Squadron from RAF Deversoir, part of the air defence force for the Canal Zone in formation over the Egyptian desert in 1954. Following the withdrawal from Palestine in 1948, the Middle East Air Force was concentrated in overcrowded bases along the length of the Suez Canal with its new headquarters at Ismailia, though its presence there was short-lived. In September 1954, 213 Squadron was one of the first squadrons to be disbanded during the long withdrawal from the Canal Zone, re-forming in Germany in 1955 equipped with the Canberra B(I)6. The Vampire fighter-bomber was widely used overseas on operations during the late 1940s and early 1950s, most notably in Malaya by 45 and 60 Squadrons and by 8 Squadron in Kenya during the Mau Mau emergency. *(RAF-T 6)*

An Iraqi coup on 14 July 1958 threatened to spill over into Jordan. Under Operation *Fortitude*, Hastings along with Beverleys and Comets moved 16th Independent Parachute Brigade Group from Cyprus to Amman to boost Jordan's defences. Six Hunter F.6s from 208 Squadron, seen here at Amman airfield, and a dozen pilots and sixty airmen were despatched from Nicosia in Cyprus to provide air cover for the brigade group. Despite having withdrawn from Jordan just thirteen months previously, the airmen were faced with little accommodation and no services until Transport Command was able to bring them in from Cyprus. Until former RAF buildings could be utilized, accommodation comprised portable huts and the operations facilities were tents at the side of the airfield. *(RAF-T 723)*

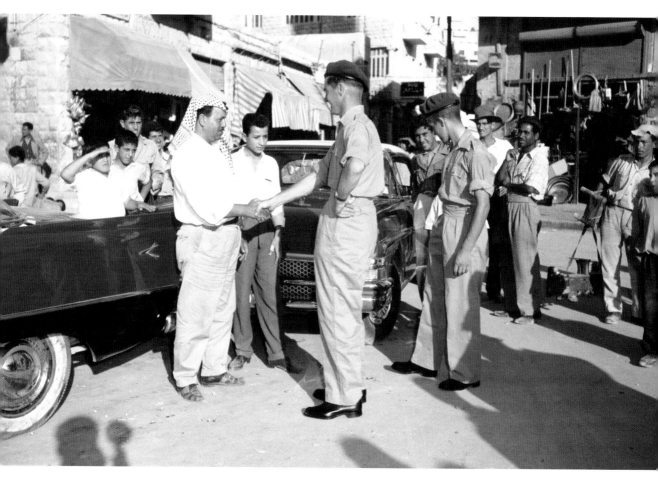

After the Suez campaign, anti-British and pro-Arab feelings led to increased hostility towards British personnel serving in the Middle East. Even in Jordan, traditionally considered an ally in the region, tensions ran high and the RAF stations at Amman and Mufraq were besieged by the local civilian population. This hostility contributed to the termination of the Anglo-Jordan treaty and hastened the RAF's withdrawal from the country. Following Operation *Fortitude*, relations improved enough to allow the airmen from 208 Squadron to once again explore Amman's old town in relative safety. The RAF left Jordan for good in October 1958. *(RAF-T 739)*

Flight Lieutenant Ken Allan, the navigation officer at RAF Lyneham, records the Flight Information Regions in the station's Operations Room c. March 1957. Though troopships continued to operate until late 1962, RAF personnel and their families were increasingly transported by aircraft. In the early 1950s, a flight to Singapore by Hastings took five days, including overnight stops at staging posts including El Adem, Habbaniya, Mauripur, or Negombo. Roger Annett, a co-pilot with 215 Squadron, recalled: 'It was like a flight through the old British Empire because we went to these RAF stations which are now like Meccas of oil riches in the Middle East, were then just tin shacks with RAF guys manning them.' In the mid-1950s the loss of these stations caused concern. At the same time, longer-ranged Comets and Britannias were entering service, but aircraft still faced a journey across the Indian Ocean, well beyond their range. (RAF-T 505)

Comet C.2 XK715 'Columba' of 216 Squadron flying from RAF Lyneham is turned around at RAF Gan in 1962. Following the loss of the Middle East air stations, the island of Gan, situated within the Maldives in the Indian Ocean, was a vital staging post for flights to the Far East. From 1957, Gan grew from a simple airstrip with few comforts to a major staging post for all aircraft flying east, offering vastly improved facilities for passengers and station staff alike. In the first year of operations, Gan handled 630 aircraft and over 12,000 passengers. By the late 1960s between 6,000 and 7,000 passengers passed through RAF Gan each month. The Comet's flight from Lyneham would also have stopped at RAF El Adem in Libya and RAF Khormaksar in Aden before flying on to Changi. As well as transport aircraft, Gan also serviced fighters and bombers heading to Far East Air Force. (RAF-T 3301)

Passengers disembark from an Air Support Command VC10, before heading to the Blue Lagoon transit hotel at RAF Gan, watched by RAF personnel in 1969. As an unaccompanied posting, no women worked or lived on Gan. As such, transport aircraft carrying servicewomen or service families on their way to Singapore often attracted the attention of the station personnel. Roger Annett, who passed through Gan on his way to join 215 Squadron in Singapore, was amazed at the men's reaction to the female passengers: *'Gan was interesting … It was 1963 and the mini-skirt was coming in … I can remember the ground crew at Gan being quite amazed at the shortness of the skirts.'* (RAF-T 8058)

A senior aircraftman and his family are served an in-flight meal by a WRAF air quartermaster sergeant on board a Comet C.2 of 216 Squadron, c. 1961. If married and over 21 years of age, a serviceman posted for a two and a half year tour to one of the larger developed stations in Cyprus, Singapore, Aden or North Africa could be 'accompanied' by his family. Shorter one-year tours or to smaller underdeveloped stations were usually 'unaccompanied'. For married servicemen, a one-year unaccompanied posting to a remote or undesirable posting such as Gan or Bahrain, might be combined with a further eighteen months at an accompanied station. National servicemen and those married but younger than 21 years of age were not entitled to take their families with them overseas (RAF-T 2261).

A pilot officer and his family leave their married quarter in Changi, Singapore, November 1958. At accompanied stations, where many RAF families were present, a wide range of facilities and accommodation were available. Married quarters were allocated on a system of 'points', which reflected the applicant's rank, any previous unaccompanied tours and the number of children in his family. When not entitled to a married quarter or where one was not available, a nearby 'hiring' (a private property rented by the RAF) could be acquired. In Singapore, with the overseas living allowance supplementing pay, a local servant or 'amah' were affordable to most personnel. Although not paid for by the RAF, many service families employed an 'amah' to help run the house. *(RAF-T 774)*

RAF personnel employing the services of a trishaw driver outside the NAAFI-run Britannia Club, opposite Raffles Hotel, Beach Road Singapore, c. 1965. For many an overseas tour was their first experience of foreign travel. The more popular postings were two-year tours to Cyprus and the Far East where developed stations contained all the facilities of home service. Singapore's vibrant and varied culture gave personnel the opportunity to experience new places, new customs and new food. A number of military social clubs, such as the Britannia and the Changi Officers' Club offered swimming, entertainment and good food. Eric Dick, an air traffic controller at RAF Changi, reflects on life in the FEAF: *'Singapore was delightful… It was a good social life, and the workload was very, very light and nothing near like I had been used to on fighter airfields at home.' (RAF-T 5283)*

Two Vulcan B.1s of 83 Squadron on an Operation *Profiteer* detachment to RAAF Butterworth, Penang, Malaya, during the Malayan Emergency, c. June 1958. Every three months between October 1957 and June 1960, two V-bombers and six crews were detached to the region for a period of two weeks. Initially undertaken by 214 Squadron's Valiants at RAF Changi, from June 1958, Vulcans were detached to RAAF Butterworth, the first being from 83 Squadron. Neither the Valiant nor the Vulcan were used operationally during the Emergency, but were considered a visible reinforcement of local units and were made available to SEATO. The Victor would later maintain a similar deployment during the Indonesian Confrontation. XA905, on the left, was the first Vulcan to be delivered to squadron service. It arrived at 83 Squadron at RAF Waddington on 11 July 1957. *(RAF-T 764)*

Despatchers of the Royal Army Service Corps load a Land Rover of the 1st Guards Brigade into a Beverley heavy-load transport during Exercise Starlight, near RAF El Adem, Libya, March 1960. El Adem, situated near Tobruk, was a hub for Transport Command exercises. In March 1960, Exercise Starlight, tested the RAF's ability to supply an advancing army solely by air. During the exercise twelve Beverleys of 47 and 53 Squadrons from RAF Abingdon undertook 194 sorties transporting 3,329 Guardsmen and 272 RAF personnel, 370 vehicles, 272 trailers, 40 guns and 1,546,559lb of freight from El Adem to an airhead at Tmimi. Pioneers and Whirlwinds then provided the troops with landed supplies, followed by the Beverleys undertaking air drops. RAF El Adem was also a major staging post for aircraft heading to the Middle East and Far East. It closed when the RAF left Libya in 1969 following a revolution in the country. *(RAF-T 1716)*

Three airmen from 37 (Field) Squadron, RAF Regiment, each armed with a L1A1 Self-Loading Rifle, man a piquet in the mountains overlooking the airfield at Thumeir, Aden, c. May 1964. From May to June 1964, RADFORCE, a force comprising Royal Marines, British Army and RAF personnel, was dispatched from Aden to pacify a Yemeni inspired rebellion in the Radfan region of South Arabia. RADFORCE assembled its headquarters at the small airfield of Thumeir, fifty miles from the Yemeni border. There it received supplies and reinforcements from RAF Khormaksar by Beverleys of 84 Squadron and Argosies of 105 Squadron. Forward positions were resupplied by Belvederes of 26 Squadron and Whirlwinds from RAF Khormaksar's Search and Rescue Flight. In addition to their traditional role of airfield defence, the RAF Regiment was also used in an infantry role, providing additional ground forces for the operation. *(RAF-T 4583)*

Flight Lieutenant Roger Pyrah, commanding officer of 1417 Flight, climbs into his Hunter FR.10 at RAF Khormaksar before undertaking a tactical photographic reconnaissance flight over Radfan, July 1964. No. 1417 Flight was established with four Hunter FR.10s in May 1963, to provide tactical reconnaissance on behalf of the pilots of ground attack Hunter FGA.9s from 8, 208 and 43 Squadrons. During 1964, the flight's first full operational year, 300 sorties were flown and over 13,000 photographs were taken of the local terrain and potential targets of opportunity. In addition to missions over Radfan, 1417 Flight was engaged in other reconnaissance duties in the region, including photographing Soviet shipping in the Gulf of Aden. *(RAF-T 4657)*

Hunter FGA.9 XG256 of 8 Squadron, armed with sixteen 20lb rockets and four 30mm Aden cannons is seen on a sortie during operations in the Radfan region, June 1964. In support of RADFORCE, the Hunters of 8, 208 and 43 Squadrons undertook strikes against pre-planned and opportunistic targets, and also provided air cover for transports ferrying troops and supplies between Khormaksar and Thumeir. Each day at RAF Khormaksar, six 8 Squadron pilots were held at ten or thirty minutes' readiness to respond to requests for air support or to undertake air defence duties. No fewer than 128 sorties were flown by 8 Squadron in June 1964 alone. This squadron had been associated with Aden since before the war, and returned in 1946 equipped with Mosquito Mk.VIs, receiving Hunter FGA.9s in 1960. In August 1967, during the evacuation of Aden, it was transferred to RAF Muharraq in Bahrain in August 1967. *(RAF-T 4624)*

RAF personnel and members of Princess Mary's Royal Air Force Nursing Service walk along Al Nahdha Road in the Steamer Point district of Aden, July 1964. The convivial scene belies the experiences of many servicemen in the protectorate. Junior Technician David Branchett was posted to Aden in 1964: 'We arrived at Khormaksar and did not like what we found. The average temperature was around 95 degrees, which exactly matched the humidity … there was a lot of sand, a lot of rock and the rest was concrete … The temperature, the flies, the smells and the all evading sand meant that when my tour was completed I could not get on the aircraft fast enough, I hated Aden.' From 1964 nationalists conducted a campaign of bombings, shootings and grenade attacks against military personnel and their families. On 19 August 1967 alone, as the RAF prepared to pull out of Khormaksar, three airmen were killed by snipers. (RAF-T 4818)

Canberra B.16 WT303 of 249 Squadron is seen being 'bombed up' at RAF Tengah while on detachment from the Near East Air Force Strike Wing at Akrotiri, between May and August 1965. In May 1955 during the Malayan Emergency, Canberra B.6s of 101 Squadron deployed to RAF Changi, the RAF's first jet bombers to go into combat. Later, Canberra squadrons from Germany and Cyprus were regularly deployed to reinforce local units during times of tension; 59 Squadron from Germany was sent to British Honduras in 1958, while 213 and 88 Squadrons went to Kuwait in 1961. During the Indonesian Confrontation, rotating deployments of all RAFG squadrons were sent to Kuantan in Malaysia while squadrons from Akrotiri went to Tengah. With navigation over the Borneo jungle difficult, the Canberras were rarely used for fear of provoking an escalation in the conflict by crossing the border into Indonesia. However, their presence deterred the Indonesians from increasing their campaign against Malaysia. (RAF-T 5204)

Victor B.1A XH588 of the Honington Wing seen in flight over the Malaysian jungle in 1965 on an Operation *Chamfrom* deployment to RAF Tengah during the Indonesian Confrontation. Following the success of *Profiteer* detachments by Valiants and Vulcans during the Malayan Emergency, under *Chamfrom* four V-bombers were sent to Singapore to provide a show of potential retaliatory force, should the Indonesian Air Force decide to strike targets on mainland Malaysia. From December 1963, Victors and Vulcans were deployed to Butterworth and Tengah. During Operation *Chamfrom* deployment crews trained in the peculiar climatic conditions of the Far East, testing Singapore air defences and training on the Song Song bombing range. *(RAF-T 5295)*

Argosy XP448 of 215 Squadron is guided into position at RAF Labuan during the Indonesian Confrontation, 1964. The crew of an Argosy consisted of a captain, co-pilot, navigator, flight engineer and air quartermaster. The air quartermaster supervised the Royal Army Service Corps air despatchers in the correct loading and dropping of the eight, one-ton containers carried by the Argosy. Piloting the aircraft to the drop zones, often located in steep river valleys in the jungle or mountains, was no easy feat. Roger Arnett, co-pilot of an Argosy remembers: *'The co-pilot has nothing to do but sit there and be terrified. You just sat there and watched the jungle go by. The jungles could got very, very close, you could see the monkeys in the trees, you could see every leaf … you are really flying at the limits … you must never let it become routine otherwise the jungle or the cloud would catch you out.'* (RAF-T 5162)

Whirlwind HAR.10 XP340 of 225 Squadron is seen landing on a temporary pad at the forward airfield at Sepulot, Sabah, Borneo, in 1964. Pioneer XL665 of 209 Squadron can be seen in the background. Throughout the Indonesian Confrontation helicopters were invaluable. Whirlwinds from 103, 110 and 230 Squadrons were detached to a number of small forward airstrips from where they would transport communications, men and supplies to and evacuate casualties from the forward positions deep in the Borneo jungle, inaccessible to most fixed wing aircraft. Supporting the Whirlwinds were heavy lift Belvederes of 66 Squadron based at Kuching. In 1964, the three burdened helicopter squadrons were reinforced from the UK by Whirlwinds of 225 Squadron, and an additional four Belvederes from 26 Squadron. *(RAF-T 5245)*

A Shackleton MR.2 WG530 of 205 Squadron is seen flying over remote jungle on Borneo whilst on a patrol in 1964. Throughout the Indonesian Confrontation, the RAF Changi-based Shackleton squadron continued its usual maritime reconnaissance work, undertaking regular anti-piracy patrols, particularly around the north coast of Sabah where there had been a growth in Philippine inspired raids. Though commonly operating over water, Shackletons of 205 Squadron also performed reconnaissance over the jungles of Borneo and mainland Malaysia to search for evidence of infiltration by Indonesian forces. In April 1964, it was a 205 Squadron Shackleton that observed parachutes in the jungle canopy near Lapis, proving that Indonesian regular troops, rather than paramilitaries, had landed on mainland Malaysia. *(RAF-T 5271)*

A crewmember of Canberra B.15 WH959 of 73 Squadron, part of the Near East Air Force Strike Wing based at Akrotiri, checks one of his aircraft's AS30 missiles during exercises at El Adem, c. 1967. The only bombers assigned to CENTO, the Canberras of the Akrotiri Strike Wing were initially armed with 1,000lb bombs stored internally and wing mounted 2-inch rockets. They later received the advanced AS30, an advanced air-to-surface missile. In 1961, Red Beard was issued to the Strike Wing, giving CENTO a nuclear capability. Part of the Strike Wing's training involved familiarization of terrain in the region, done by Lone Ranger flights or navigation exercises (Navex) to signatory states such as Iran and Pakistan. Canberra crews also frequently exercised with NATO and CENTO forces in the Mediterranean. LABS manoeuvre or bomb and rocket live fire exercises on the ranges at El Adem were also conducted. (RAF-T 6881)

Javelin FAW.9Rs of 64 Squadron on an air-defence patrol over Malaysia in May 1967. In early 1964, with Indonesian aircraft frequently crossing the border into Malaysian airspace an Air Defence Identification Zone was established over Borneo and mainland Malaysia. Policing it were Hunter FGA.9s from 20 Squadron and Javelins FAW.9Rs of 60 Squadron based at RAF Tengah, with detached aircraft deployed at Labuan and Kuching. No. 64 Squadron joined them from RAF Waterbeach in September 1964. Detachments of Javelins at RAAF Butterworth patrolled over north western Malaysia, while at Singapore crews maintained QRA to respond to infiltrating Indonesian aircraft. In 1964, an Indonesian Air Force Hercules crashed while being pursued by a Javelin of 60 Squadron. (RAF-T 7074)

Lightning F.3s XR720 and XP748 of 56 Squadron armed with Firestreak missiles and with pilots seated in the cockpit are seen on the ORP undertaking QRA at RAF Akrotiri in 1967. During the Arab-Israeli war and with tension between Greece and Turkey, in April 1967, 56 Squadron deployed to Akrotiri to provide the island's air defence. Under CENTO obligations the squadron held at least two aircraft at ten-minute readiness to respond to threats to the island's bases. Air Chief Marshal Michael Graydon was at the time the OC of 56 Squadron: *'We only had eighteen pilots holding a twenty-four hour alert. We used to do it for periods of a month on and then a month off. That's very demanding. It was not uncommon to be doing a 70 or 80 hour week … Overnight, when you were on alert you weren't doing anything, just staying awake, but it was very tiring.'* (RAF-T 7467)

Chapter Four

Aircraft

At the end of the Second World War, the RAF had on strength over 9,000 front-line aircraft. By the summer of 1948, three years of post-war contraction had reduced this to 1,100. The rearmament and expansion that followed the Berlin Blockade intensified at the outbreak of the Korean War and by 1952, the number of aircraft had grown to 1,700. Yet, until the introduction of new types, the RAF's inventory consisted of a growing number of largely inadequate aircraft. Many of the new aircraft being introduced from the mid-1950s brought vastly improved capability across the commands. Successive defence cuts after 1957 saw aircraft acquired in increasingly smaller numbers, reversing the growth of previous years. By 1969, the total number of combat aircraft had fallen to 750, less than half of its 1952 peak.

From 1948 until 1954, the RAF's expansion was characterized by an increase in size if not in capability. Fighter Command squadrons increasingly converted to the wartime jet Meteor and Vampire and by 1952, following the introduction of these aircraft as night fighters, Fighter Command was fully jet equipped. Until 1954, the principal day fighter was the Meteor F.8, serving with thirty Fighter Command and RAuxAF squadrons. However, flown by the Royal Australian Air Force over Korea, the Meteor was found to be inadequate against the fast and manoeuvrable MiG-15. Consequently, it only served in UK air defence squadrons where it would face slow Soviet bombers, and never equipped front-line units in Germany. Instead, in 1953 under the Mutual Defence Aid Programme (MDAP), 428 battle-proven Sabre F.4s were acquired, equipping ten squadrons in 2TAF. Joining it, the Vampire was redeveloped as a fighter-bomber, later supplemented by the Venom, and issued primarily to squadrons in Germany and overseas commands.

In 1947, the Avro Lancaster MR.3 was the RAF's principal long-range maritime reconnaissance aircraft, aided until 1959 by Sunderland flying boats. Responding to a growth in the Soviet Navy, the aging Lancaster was replaced from February 1951 by the Avro Shackleton MR.1, a maritime derivative of the Lincoln bomber. The Shackleton operated in maritime reconnaissance, anti-submarine and search and rescue roles for nearly twenty years. Despite being the RAF's last four-piston engine aircraft with wartime ancestry, the Shackleton proved popular as a hard-working and robust, if high-maintenance, aircraft.

During these early years, only Bomber Command transformed in a way required as it entered the Cold War. In 1950, 600 wartime-designed Avro Lincoln medium bombers provided the RAF's main offensive capability. With a 14,000lb payload, the slow Lincoln proved useful in low-intensity conflicts in Malaya and Kenya, but was inadequate for European service. Partially replacing the Lincoln, the RAF introduced the Canberra, its first jet bomber and a massive evolution in bomber technology. Developed to be a fast unarmed light bomber, the Canberra had a speed of over 500 miles per hour, nearly double that of the Lincoln, and a ceiling of 48,000ft, enabling the Canberra to operate beyond the reach of any contemporary interceptor. In May 1951, the first of over 400 Canberra B.2s entered service, equipping thirty-five squadrons by 1955.

The mid-1950s saw a period of significant re-equipment, with many of the RAF's new aircraft becoming icons of the Cold War. The introduction to service of the Hunter F.1 day fighter in July 1954 began the modernization of Fighter Command. The fast manoeuvrable swept-wing Hunter was immediately popular with pilots. A later variant, the Hunter F.6, had a speed of Mach 0.95 and a ceiling of 50,000ft, enabling it to intercept the previously invulnerable Canberra during exercises. By 1959, over 1,000 Hunters had been delivered, serving in thirty-one squadrons, superseding the Meteor in the UK and the Sabre in Germany. The Hunter FGA.9, with wing-mounted bombs and rockets, was an effective ground attack aircraft replacing the Venom.

Operating alongside the Hunter in the night fighter role was the Javelin, the RAF's only delta-winged fighter. Beset by development problems, the FAW.1 prematurely entered service in February 1956, with equally flawed versions following. The introduction in 1959 of the FAW.7, with improved engines, additional fuel capacity and for the first time air-to-air missiles, finally saw the Javelin become an effective interceptor. Yet, difficult to maintain and having a tendency to catch fire on start-up, the Javelin was generally unpopular with ground crews.

Between January 1955 and November 1957, the iconic V-Force entered service. Replacing the obsolete Lincoln, these four jet engine aircraft provided Bomber Command with a previously lacking long-range nuclear capability. While the Valiant was conservatively designed, the revolutionary delta-winged Vulcan and the swept-wing Victor had extraordinary performance. Speeds between Mach 0.92 and 0.98, faster than most contemporary fighters, a range of over 4,500 miles and a height ceiling of 55,000ft, initially protected them from interception. Superseded, the versatile Canberra made a successful conversion to the interdictor and tactical strike roles serving in Germany until 1972.

From the mid-1950s, Transport Command upgraded both its strategic and tactical aircraft. From 1948, long-distance transport had been provided by the Handley Page Hastings, a stalwart of Transport Command but one that was increasingly inadequate. Replacing it were two modified civil airliners, offering a significantly improved capability to rapidly deploy an army around the world. From July 1956, the de Havilland Comet, the RAF's first jet transport, was introduced to fly the strategic routes to Aden and Singapore. Carrying forty-four passengers, the Comet took just thirty-eight hours to reach Singapore, rather than five days by Hastings. In 1959, the Comet was joined by the Bristol Britannia. With a maximum range of 5,000 miles, the Britannia transported up to 115 troops or fifty-three stretcher cases along with heavy cargo over the key routes to overseas stations.

The introduction of the short-range, heavy-lift Blackburn Beverley in March 1956 provided the RAF with a capable tactical transport. Over short distances, the Beverley could carry up to ninety passengers, seventy paratroopers or a payload of 20 tons (44,000lb), which for the first time could be loaded and dropped from the rear fuselage. Introduced in 1955, the Whirlwind HAR.2 and later HAR.10 helicopters boosted the capability of both Transport Command and Coastal Command in the light-lift and SAR role.

In 1960, Fighter Command received an interceptor, the performance of which was beyond anything then in service. With a speed of over Mach 2, more than twice the speed of the Hunter, the technologically advanced Lightning was the RAF's first truly supersonic aircraft. Its initial climb rate of 50,000ft per minute and ceiling of over 60,000ft made it an exceptional interceptor. Hampered by a characteristic short range, the addition of a refuelling probe along with overwing tanks and a larger ventral fuel tank in later versions doubled its fuel capacity. Immensely popular with pilots, ground crew and public alike, the Lightning became one of the most iconic British aircraft of the Cold War.

By the early 1960s, with Britain engaged in several conflicts around the world, the RAF sought to increase Transport Command's ability to quickly move troops. Comet C.4s entered service from 1962, carrying more passengers at a greater speed than the earlier Comet C.2s. That year, the Armstrong Whitworth Argosy was also acquired as a medium-range, medium lift transport, replacing the long serving Hastings, which had been relegated to the tactical role since the introduction of the Britannia. From 1966, the Vickers VC10, the third of the RAF's converted airliners, which could carry 150 passengers to Singapore in just nineteen hours, began to replace the Comet on the routes east.

In 1957, the Defence White Paper cancelled all fighter programmes after the Lightning. When the all-missile air-defences predicted in the White Paper did not materialize development recommenced. Following budget cuts, the proposed P.1154 supersonic V/STOL aircraft was cancelled in 1965. This left the RAF with no successor to the Lightning or the Hunter FGA.9. With the cost of developing purely British aircraft becoming prohibitive, the RAF turned to the United States and purchased two variants of the long-range and heavily armed McDonnell Douglas Phantom. The Phantom FG.1 entered service in September 1969, serving as an air defence interceptor alongside the Lightning, until the latter's retirement in 1988. The Phantom was retired in 1992.

In May 1969, the supersonic Phantom FGR.2 superseded the Hunter FGA.9 in the ground attack role. Joining it operationally from January 1970 was the subsonic Hawker Siddeley Harrier GR.1, the world's first V/STOL combat aircraft. By 1972, four squadrons of Harriers were operating in the UK and Germany. Like the Lightning in the UK, the Harrier in Germany came to symbolize operations during the second half of the Cold War.

The cuts of 1965 also cancelled the highly advanced TSR.2, a Mach 2, tactical strike and reconnaissance aircraft destined to supersede the Canberra B(I)8s. In 1967, further cuts resulted in the cancellation of the TSR.2's successor, the General Dynamics F.111. Reluctantly, the RAF accepted the Hawker Siddeley Buccaneer, a subsonic low level strike aircraft that had been in service with the Royal Navy since 1962. The first aircraft entered squadron service in October 1969, taking its place in Germany as a front-line strike aircraft the following year. Initially an unpopular choice, the Buccaneer proved adept at low level and became popular with pilots, remaining in service until 1994.

Following the withdrawal from Singapore in 1971, the RAF's vast transport fleets were no longer required. Consequently while the VC10 continued, the Comet C.4 retired in 1975 and the Britannia in 1976. With the last Argosys due to retire in the mid-1970s, attention again turned to the United States, this time for a tactical transport. In August 1967, the first Lockheed C-130 Hercules C.1 entered service and by mid-1968, there were five squadrons. The last two long-serving Hercules from the 1967 batch finally retired in October 2013. The successor Hercules C.4 and C.5 are expected to continue well into the twenty-first century.

Armstrong Whitworth Meteor NF.14 WS848 of Fighter Command Comunications Squadron based at RAF Bovingdon in flight on 17 August 1960. In 1951, with the Gloster Aircraft Company producing the Javelin, the production of the night fighter variant of the Meteor was undertaken by Armstrong Whitworth. The main visible differences between the night and day fighters included lengthened wings, an elongated nose, which held the radar, and a second seat for the radar operator / navigator. NF.14s entered service with 25 Squadron at RAF West Malling in March 1954. They were withdrawn from 1956 following the delivery of the Javelin. NF.14s remained in service overseas with 60 Squadron in Singapore until 1961. Meteor NF.14 WS848, the last Meteor to be built, did not see front-line service. In September 1955, following four months with the Central Fighter Establishment at West Raynham it transferred to FCCS where it served until 1962. It was struck off at 33 Maintenance Unit in February 1963. *(RAF-T 2094)*

Six Canberra PR.9s from 58 Squadron, and their crews, at RAF Wyton in September 1960. In January that year, 58 Squadron become the first unit to receive the PR.9, an improved version of the useful photographic reconnaissance aircraft. The Canberra PR.3, introduced in 1952, was the RAF's first purely photographic reconnaissance aircraft. Cameras within its three camera bays enabled it to undertake high and low altitude, oblique and vertical, day and night photography. In 1953, 58 Squadron moved to Wyton, home of the RAF's Strategic Reconnaissance Force, where they were later joined by Valiant B(PR).1s of 543 Squadron. In October 1962, during the Cuban Missile Crisis, the squadron photographed Soviet shipping movements in the North Atlantic. The squadron disbanded in September 1970. The last PR.9 left RAF service in 2006. To the right of the image, in the distance, can be seen one of 543 Squadron's Valiants. *(RAF-T 2100)*

Two Supermarine Swift FR.5s, WK281 and XD913 of 79 Squadron, seen in starboard echelon formation, with Hunter F.6s of 14 and 26 Squadrons of the Gütersloh Wing, June 1960. The Swift F.1, the RAF's first swept-wing interceptor, was first introduced into service with 56 Squadron in February 1954. The Swift interceptor was a disappointment and after several fatal crashes the aircraft was withdrawn in May 1955. Proving more successful, the tactical reconnaissance version, the Swift FR.5, entered service in 1956 equipping 2 and 79 Squadrons of 2TAF in Germany for five years. The Swift FR.5s of 79 Squadron were replaced by Hunter FR.10s in January 1961, with 2 Squadron reequipping soon after. In June 1960, shortly after this photograph was taken, XD913 was struck off charge following a forced landing at RAF Gütersloh when its nose wheel failed to lower. *(RAF-T 1887)*

Hawker Hunter F.5 WP183 of 56 Squadron in flight from RAF Waterbeach, 16 April 1956. Like many British post-war fighters, the Hunter was initially underpowered and short on range. By the F.6 version, it had become an outstanding aircraft. To those who flew it, it was superb in reliability and handling and beautiful in appearance. Alan Pollock, a pilot with 1 Squadron, believed that the Hunter was: '… *marvellous. You really felt as a 20-year-old that you'd drawn the long straw of life to fly the Hunter in those days, because it was something special.'* In front-line service between 1954 and 1971, the Hunter is one of the most iconic aircraft of the Cold War. *(RAF-T 37)*

Javelin FAW.1s XA624, XA568 and XA618 of 46 Squadron based at RAF Odiham, display for the photographer, 2 July 1956. The revolutionary Javelin was the RAF's only delta-wing interceptor and the first to be equipped with air-to-air missiles. It was incredibly heavy, weighing nearly twenty tons, but with engines initially underpowered, its performance was sluggish. Air Chief Marshal Richard Johns: '*The early marks of Javelin were grotesquely underpowered, but you could learn the job on it... I was posted to 64 Squadron at Duxford, where they had the Javelin 9s, a serious leap, by then a seriously good night fighter. I mean it did have some quirks, but in its day it was the heaviest armed all-weather fighter in the world.*' Javelins served with Fighter Command until October 1964 and RAF Germany until 1966. *(RAF-T 307)*

Two Lightning F.3s, XP702 and XP751, of 74 Squadron are seen in flight over St Andrews shortly after the squadron moved to RAF Leuchars in 1964. Each aircraft is armed with two Firestreak missiles. A formidable aircraft, the Lightning was the first interceptor to be designed as an integrated weapons system rather than a gun platform. Its Airborne Interception (AI) radar could track and lock on a target, arm the missiles, and indicate to the pilot to fire while the target was still out of sight. They were, however, lightly armed carrying just two missiles. The 30mm Aden cannon present in the F.1 was removed from the F.3 onwards, and replaced by an optional gun pack in the belly on the F.6. The F.3 was the most widely issued variant of the Lightning, with seventy-one entering service. No. 74 Squadron was the first squadron to receive the aircraft in April 1964, with XP751 and XP702 being the second and third to be delivered. *(RAF-T 4800)*

Shackleton MR.2 WR960 of 228 Squadron, RAF St Mawgan, flying low over the water near Longships Lighthouse off the Cornish coast, c. 1957. The Shackleton's tailplane and twin fins are evidence of its Avro heritage. A versatile and robust aircraft, the Shackleton was in service from 1951 until 1991, almost the entire Cold War. Principally, operating from Britain in the maritime reconnaissance and anti-submarine role, Shackletons were also used in the Middle East and Far East in the search and rescue and anti-piracy roles. From 1971, twelve MR.2s were converted to AEW.2 airborne early warning aircraft to provide early warning radar coverage over the northern Atlantic Ocean. The Shackleton's high maintenance nature and the noise of its Griffon engines gave rise to it being affectionately known as '10,000 rivets flying in close formation' and 'the Growler'. (RAF-T 326)

An unidentified Valiant B.1 being serviced at RAF Wittering, August 1956. When introduced, the Valiant was the most advanced aircraft in the RAF's inventory. To Air Vice-Marshal Hazelwood, Commanding Officer of 90 Squadron, the Valiant was a: *'super aircraft, I got to love the Valiant so did all of the other pilots. No doubt in my mind, first rate British aircraft; designed by British chaps, produced by British chaps and flown by British pilots. Certainly in my opinion it was one of the best aircraft I ever flew.'* It was the only aircraft of the V-Force to be designed with a dual role as bomber, strategic reconnaissance and air-to-air refueller from the outset. However, compared with the Vulcan and the Victor, the Valiant's design was more conservative and with a top speed of Mach 0.82 (567mph) at 37,000ft its performance was more modest. *(RAF-T 98)*

Vulcan B.1 XH497 from 617 Squadron at RAF Scampton, banks away from the camera highlighting her delta-wing, 10 November 1958. The Vulcan is probably the most recognized of all RAF aircraft from the Cold War. Produced in greater number than the Valiant and the Victor, forty five B.1s were produced between February 1957 and March 1959. Even as the last Vulcan B.1 became operational, the improved B.2 was well into production, with eighty-nine being built, the first entering service with 230 OCU in August 1960. This variant had the highest performance of all the V-bombers with a maximum speed of Mach 0.98 (746mph) and a ceiling of 60,000ft. The final Vulcan B.2 off the production line entered service with 35 Squadron in January 1965, just after the Valiant was withdrawn. XH558, the last in service, was retired in March 1993. XH497 was delivered to 617 Squadron in May 1958. It was scrapped in 1969 while serving with 50 Squadron. *(RAF-T 717)*

Victor B.1 XA936 of 10 Squadron seen during a flight from RAF Cottesmore in September 1958. The last of the V-bombers, the Victor was the largest, heaviest and most aerodynamic of the force. Incredibly, a Victor B.1 accidentally became the largest aircraft to break the sound barrier, doing so whilst in a shallow dive during a test flight in 1957. The first operational unit to receive the Victor B.1 in April 1958 was 10 Squadron, followed by 15, 55 and 57 Squadrons. Like the Vulcan, a more powerful B.2 variant was produced with thirty-four entering service from February 1962. XA936 later served with XV Squadron before being converted to a K.1 refuelling tanker. *(RAF-T 686)*

Hastings C.1 TG587 of 511 Squadron taxies across a dusty airfield at Amman, Jordan, during Operation *Fortitude* in July 1958. With a range of approximately 1,700 miles and the ability to carry up to fifty troops, the Hastings had, since its introduction in 1948, proved valuable as the RAF's principal strategic transport. In total 100 Hastings were issued to eleven Transport Command squadrons, one Coastal Command squadron as well as the Middle East and Far East air forces. In September 1958, 511 Squadron disbanded to be reformed in December 1959 equipped with the Britannia. With the introduction of the Britannia, the RAF's remaining Hastings assumed a tactical role until replaced by the Argosy. *(RAF-T 725)*

Beverley C.1 XB284 of 47 Squadron based at RAF Abingdon, c. 1957. At the time of its introduction in March 1956, the Beverley was the largest aircraft ever operated by the RAF. It became the backbone of RAF tactical transport during the late 1950s and early 1960s. Forty-seven were delivered, serving with 30, 47 and 53 Squadrons based at RAF Abingdon, 34 Squadron at RAF Seletar in Singapore and 84 Squadron at RAF Khormaksar in Aden. For its size, it had a remarkable short take-off and landing capability, which proved useful when operating during the campaigns in Borneo and Aden. Air drops could be made from the rear of the fuselage, for which the doors were removed pre-flight, while parachute troops could also be dropped from a hatch in the tail boom. XB284 was transferred to 84 Squadron in July 1967. In September 1967, all remaining Beverleys, including XB284, were retired and struck off charge. *(RAF-T 423)*

Officer Commanding 216 Squadron at RAF Lyneham, Wing Commander W. I. Harris AFC, and the flight-engineer of Comet C.2 XK697 'Cygnus', are seen in discussion in March 1957. Introduced in June 1956, by November Comets of 216 Squadron were running monthly services to Aden and Singapore. That year, the squadron also moved troops to Malta and Cyprus in response to the Suez Crisis and the Cyprus Emergency. From 1962, the larger Comet C.4 was able to carry ninety-four passengers to Singapore in twenty-four hours, a significant improvement on the C.2. The Comet was often noted for its comfort. From *Flight* magazine in 1956: *'Up front the interior noise was mechanical, reminiscent of a power station. Aft the noise was all jet, but neither factor prevented the Comet being synonymous with comfort.'* In 1967, XK697 was transferred to 51 Squadron of Signals Command to undertake Electrical Intelligence (ELINT) work. *(RAF-T 502)*

The first Britannia C.1 in RAF service, XL636 'Argo' of 99 Squadron is seen during a flight from its base at RAF Lyneham, soon after delivery on 4 June 1959. Between June 1959 and December 1960, twenty Britannia C.1s were delivered to 99 and 511 Squadrons, later joined by three C.2s, which along with the ten Comets of 216 Squadron formed the RAF's strategic transport force during the early 1960s. The Britannia had a top speed of 400mph, a range of 5,000 miles, and could carry over 100 troops or 16 tons (36,000lb) of cargo. Frequently used for aeromedical evacuation, it could also be equipped to hold fifty-three stretchers with six medical attendants. *(RAF-T 1078)*

Twin Pioneer CC.1 XM961 of 21 Squadron based at RAF Eastleigh, Nairobi, overflies an RAF Regiment command post in the Kenyan bush, 1961. The Twin Pioneer was used for colonial policing and humanitarian operations, including in Aden, Kenya, Malaya and Borneo. It was able to carry cargo or sixteen passengers internally, or an externally slung cargo load. For policing duties, it could also be armed with Browning guns and door-mounted Bren guns and carry a small number of light bombs. With a short take-off and landing capability, the 'Twin Pin' was ideal for resupplying troops at forward airstrips. Thirty-nine Twin Pioneers were in service with six RAF squadrons. The last Twin Pioneer squadron, 209 Squadron, disbanded at RAF Seletar, Singapore in December 1968. *(RAF-T 2070)*

Argosy C.1 XN849 of the Argosy Operational Conversion Unit at RAF Benson, January 1962. Having been operated by the OCU since November 1961, from March 1962, fifty-six Argosies were delivered to six RAF squadrons, operating in the UK and overseas in the medium-lift transport role. The Argosy's high twin tail boom and clam-shell rear doors gave air quartermasters the ability to rapidly load vehicles and freight. Unlike the Beverley, the Argosy's rear doors could be opened electronically during flight to enable airdrops. Parachute troops could also be dropped from side doors in the fuselage. Argosy E.1s, were supplied as radar calibration aircraft to 115 Squadron within 90 (Signals) Group at RAF Brize Norton. XN849 later served with 114 Squadron at Benson and 105 Squadron in Aden. In May 1970, it passed to 5 Maintenance Unit at Kemble and was struck off charge. *(RAF-T 2884)*

Whirlwind HAR.10 XJ726 of RAF Khormaksar's search and rescue flight picks up a cargo net of supplies from Thumeir airfield, Aden, during the Radfan campaign, in May 1964. During the Malayan Emergency, 194 Squadron had shown the potential of helicopters for providing troop and supply lift, but were often hampered by reliability and performance. The third version of the Whirlwind, the HAR.10 introduced in November 1961, was an improvement on earlier versions, having a turbine engine that gave a more power and was better suited for tropical conditions, serving successfully in many overseas squadrons, particularly within the Far East. It also served with 22, 202 and 228 Squadrons within Coastal Command on search and rescue duties. HAR.10s replaced Bristol Sycamores within Khormaksar's search and rescue flight in March 1964. During the Radfan campaign, the flight provided a valuable service ferrying supplies and personnel from Khormaksar to remote airstrips such as Thumeir. (RAF-T 4631)

Local children watch as Belvedere HC.1 XG453 of 66 Squadron takes off from Krokong, Sarawak after it had transported a group of Ghurkhas to their remote village during the Indonesian Confrontation, 1964. The Belvedere provided a medium-to-heavy helicopter lift capability, supplementing the lighter Whirlwind and Wessex. It carried up to eighteen fully equipped troops, over 5,000lb of underslung cargo or 6,000lb internally. The Belvedere was widely used by 26 Squadron in Aden, but when used by 66 Squadron for service in Borneo, it suffered regular mechanical troubles and developed a reputation for unreliability and poor performance. XG453 caught fire during engine start at RAF Seleter in March 1969. In that same month the Squadron disbanded and the Belvedere was retired. *(RAF-T 5262)*

VC10 C.1 XR808 'Kenneth Campbell VC' of 10 Squadron at RAF Kai Tak following 'Flight 2300', the first scheduled troop service to Hong Kong from RAF Brize Norton on 4 April 1967. XR808 was the first of fourteen VC10s to enter RAF service, arriving on 7 July 1966. Modifications made to the airliner before it entered RAF service included a side-loading freight door, a strengthened floor, a refuelling probe and backwards-facing seats. From the early 1980s, further VC10s were acquired to act in the air-to-air refuelling role to support and then replace the Victor, which had undertaken this role since 1965. In the early 1990s, to supplement this fleet, the remaining thirteen VC10 C.1s were converted to enable a refuelling capability when it was needed. XR808 was converted to C.1K standard in October 1996. It finally retired on 29 July 2013, after forty-seven years of service. *(RAF-T 6681)*

Phantom Y F-4M XT852, the first Phantom in RAF colours, takes off at the McDonnell Douglas factory in St Louis, Missouri, for a test flight on 17 February 1967. The Phantom F-4M (designated FGR.2 in RAF service) had a performance equal to that of the Lightning and a volume of weaponry far in excess of the aging Hunter FGA.9s and the Canberras B(I)8s it replaced. Similarly, the Phantom F.4K (designated FG.1), which was purchased as an interceptor, had a range nearly 1,000 miles further than the Lightning F.6. With eight air-to-air missiles it was also more heavily armed. Received in July 1968 by 238 OCU at RAF Coltishall, the FGR.2 was introduced to squadron service with 6 Squadron in May 1969. In September that year, the first FG.1 was delivered to 43 Squadron at Leuchars. With the arrival of the Jaguar in 1974, the FGR.2s assumed interceptor duties, hastening the Lightning's withdrawal. *(RAF-T 7006)*

In a series of photographs marking its introduction to service, Hercules C.1 XV194 of 36 Squadron, Air Support Command, is seen during a flight from its base at RAF Lyneham in August 1967. The Hercules was first introduced to RAF service with 232 OCU at RAF Thorney Island in April 1967, with 36 Squadron at Lyneham became the first operational unit. Though purchased as a tactical transport, the Hercules also proved to be capable at strategic movements. By mid-1968, sixty-six aircraft were serving in four squadrons within the UK and one squadron at RAF Changi, Singapore. After just five years' service, XV194 was written off during a crash-landing at Tromsø, Norway, in 1972. (RAF-T 7598)

Hawker Siddeley Nimrod MR.1 XV226 comes into land at Farnborough during the airshow of September 1968. The design of the Nimrod utilized the airframe of the redundant Comet C.4. The Nimrods provided 18 (Maritime) Group of Strike Command with a replacement for the long-standing and hardworking Shackleton, which had been operating in the maritime reconnaissance role since 1951. In October 1971, the first Nimrod was delivered to 201 Squadron at RAF Kinloss, and at the same time, the last Shackleton MR.3 was retired. Versions of the Nimrod provided maritime reconnaissance and airborne early warning for the next thirty years. *(RAF-T 9525)*

Chapter Five

Recruitment and Training

In 1945, RAF manpower totalled 1.3 million. Within three years, demobilization had seen this figure decrease to just 202,000. In addition to the release of 'hostilities only' recruits and a freeze in recruitment, the reduction in manpower through retirement saw the loss of many experienced pre-war personnel. In 1948, with West-Soviet relations deteriorating the RAF began recruiting once more and by 1952, manpower, including National Service and short-service engagements, had reached a post-war peak of 272,000. Initially, amid concerns of poor accommodation, pay and prospects, it regularly struggled to recruit, particularly skilled tradesmen and aircrew officers on longer-term engagements.

Between 1947 and 1961, over 388,000 National Servicemen were conscripted into the RAF, accounting for over 30 per cent of personnel until the late 1950s, boosting total numbers and alleviating shortfalls in lesser-skilled trades. Two years (initially eighteen months) was insufficient to train conscripts on increasingly advanced aircraft and equipment and from the mid-1950s their use as technicians was progressively phased out. In 1949, the Women's Royal Air Force was established, providing a valuable source of manpower, reaching 10,000 members by 1953. Members of the WRAF operated alongside male counterparts in over 80 per cent of trades, though initially not in technical roles.

In January 1950, to boost recruitment, short-service engagements of three and four years were introduced. It was hoped these initial short engagements would encourage men towards permanent careers, or at least further five, ten or twelve-year engagements, as advanced technicians. To this end, pay was significantly improved for those serving nine years or over. These changes attracted recruits, but re-engagement was low and, as late as 1955, only 34 per cent of RAF personnel were on engagements of more than nine years.

By 1951, new technology entering service required men with increasingly specialist skills. In response, the RAF introduced a new trade structure of twenty-two role specific trade groups, e.g. aircraft engineering. Within each trade group roles were arranged in three levels of skill, Trade Assistants, Skilled Trades and Advanced Trades, allowing airmen an opportunity to specialize for promotion within their chosen trade group. In addition, new Command and Technician career ladders allowed progression when aptitude was stronger in either leadership or technical skills. The arrangement did not last long and the technician ranks were abolished in 1964.

As a result of these changes, men who had signed up in the early 1950s were by 1960 providing the core of the RAF's advanced technicians. In this position, and by now with sufficient recruitment, the RAF withdrew engagements of under five years. Increasingly from the mid-1950s, recruitment campaigns promoted junior entry schemes to satisfy the RAF's long-term manning requirements and provide future NCOs. Apprentices and boy entrants were, from approximately 15 years of age, intensively trained, enabling them to start their initial twelve years' service at an advanced stage. By 1960, re-engagement had improved and as the last National Serviceman demobilized in 1963, the proportion of nine-year plus engagements was now over 80 per cent. Successive cuts in the overall level of manpower after 1957, along with up-skilling of personnel and new efficient working practises, led to the majority of ground trades being adequately manned for the remainder of the decade.

From 1953, introduction to service life for all male adult non-commissioned entrants, including National Servicemen, began at No. 2 Reception Unit at RAF Cardington for induction, attestation, uniform allocation and medicals. After a short time recruits, as aircraftmen (2nd class), proceeded to one of a number of Schools of Recruit Training where, for eight weeks, they was subjected to 'square bashing' under the dreaded drill instructors, physical fitness, weapon handling and the ubiquitous 'bulling' of uniform, kit and accommodation. Here regulars would select their trade group. National Servicemen, without previous civilian experience had theirs allocated, based on the RAF's requirements.

After passing out, airmen attended a School of Technical Training for trade courses of varying length, dependant on trade, or alternatively went to an operational station for on-the-job training. Within just a few months of signing up and satisfactory completion of training, airmen were promoted to aircraftman (1st class), starting their careers. Further promotion to leading aircraftman and senior aircraftman were achievable through experience. For regular recruits, 'Part 1 Advanced Training' opened the way to Skilled Trades and promotion through NCO ranks. Passing 'Part 2 Advanced Training' qualified men to be NCOs in the higher skilled Advanced Trades in the Command or Technical streams. Occasionally, qualified airmen were identified for permanent commission as officers in a relevant branch.

Boy entrants and apprentices reported directly to the Schools of Technical Training. Basic training began with three months in an Initial Training Squadron, followed by fifteen months of general education alongside advanced trade training. On completion boy entrants usually began their career as leading aircraftmen with promotion to senior aircraftmen after six months; top boy entrants graduated as senior aircraftmen while others transferred to the Aircraft or Administrative Apprentice schemes. Aircraft apprentices undertook three years' specialist instruction after which they started their careers in engineering roles as junior technicians or corporals in Advanced Trades. Administrative apprentices in preparation for a career in accounts, supply or as clerks, followed a similar route, but on a shorter twenty-month course.

In 1965, the Boy Entrant and Aircraft Apprentice schemes were abolished and replaced by a three-year Technical Apprentice scheme for boys of 16-plus who graduated as corporals, a two-year Craft Apprenticeship for the less skilled, who started in the rank of junior technician, and a one-year Craft Apprenticeship for non-technical or administrative tradesmen who began their career as leading or senior aircraftmen. Many apprentices, and boy entrants became senior non-commissioned officers, some were selected for commission.

The loss of experienced officers after the war was equally acute. Recruiting resumed in 1948 but until a core of permanent or 'full-career' officers could be re-established, filling the gap were National Service officers and officers holding short-service or extended wartime commissions. Over the next decade, with few short-service officers reengaging after their initial commission and insufficient recruits seeking permanent commissions, the RAF encountered a worrying shortage of full-career officers, particularly experienced aircrew. In response, the RAF modified the available routes to commission and improved pay and conditions, making long-term careers more attractive.

In 1950, pilots (and later navigators) holding permanent commissions in the General Duties (GD) branch, along with officers in the Equipment and Secretarial branches, entered principally via a cadetship at the RAF College Cranwell. From 1952, technical cadets were trained at the RAF Technical College Henlow, providing the RAF's permanent technical officers. Similarly, warrant officers and chief technicians from the ground trades were commissioned as Branch Officers, thereby providing highly experienced junior officers.

For non-permanent officers, five-year short-service commissions were available in the ground branches, as were four and eight-year commissions for aircrew in the GD branch. In 1955, to increase the benefit gained from training aircrew, a Direct Entry scheme replaced short service commissions. Direct entrants were given the choice of either twelve years' service with the option of leaving after eight or a full-career to 38 years of age, and often 55, but with limited prospects of promotion.

Officers holding permanent commissions were not rank limited and the rigorous training provided by RAF colleges to develop leadership, prepared cadets for the possibility of higher rank and command, whilst introducing traditions and lifestyle expected of RAF officers. Cadetships started with four months of initial training, with the remainder of the year dedicated to academic studies, RAF law and administration, undertaking flight familiarization on Chipmunks and air navigation classes. From the second year, they advanced their academic studies, whilst commencing either branch training or flying training using the Percival Provost and Vampire or after 1960 basic jet training on the Hunting Jet Provost.

Training for the majority of RAF aircrew differed to that given to cadets at Cranwell. Lasting eighteen months, Direct Entry aircrew training focused less on academia being more akin to branch training. On completion of a sixteen-week ground course at No. 1 Initial Training School at RAF Kirton-in-Lindsey, or from 1957 at RAF South Cerney, pilot cadets progressed to Flying Training Schools for basic and advanced flying training while undertaking relevant ground classes. Navigators reported to an Air Navigation School for advanced navigation training.

On completion of training, Direct Entry and Cranwell cadets received their wings and were confirmed as pilot officers, most then proceeding to Operational Conversion Units to prepare for squadron service. Pilots destined for Transport or Coastal Commands progressed to an Advanced Flying Training School for conversion to multi-engine aircraft.

Compounding the previous years' poor recruiting, the publication of the 1957 Defence White Paper led to a dramatic drop in aircrew applicants. Faced with a shrinking, 'push-button', missile-equipped air force, a flying career was no longer seen as secure or worthwhile. Neither extensive promotion of new aircraft nor demonstrated need for bomber or transport aircrew significantly reversed this trend. The paper's effect on aircrew recruitment lasted until the mid-1960s, exacerbated by further cuts to personnel and aircraft.

An identified barrier to aircrew recruitment was long-term career prospects. Aircrew holding a permanent commission up to the rank of squadron leader initially faced retirement at the age of 43. From 1960 they were offered the option of retiring at 38 or continuing to 55, bringing the RAF into line with competing civilian recruiters. In a bid to increase aircrew applicants, five year short-service GD branch commissions were introduced. Additionally, salary and aircrew flight pay were substantially increased throughout the late 1950s and 1960s. By 1962, these measures were partially being credited for raising the number of applicants, particularly via the Direct Entry scheme, and the RAF reached its aircrew recruitment quota in that category for the first time since 1956.

Initially sourcing directly from schools, between 1950 and 1970 the RAF, in recognition of the increasing intricacy of its work, raised the educational standard and qualifications required for full-career officers. Seeking technical officers able to respond to the modernization and complexity of aircraft and weapons, from 1952 an increasing number of Technical Cadetships were undertaken at civilian universities. In 1959, to attract academically minded recruits who might otherwise have gone to university prior to employment, Cranwell's academic syllabus was raised to degree level. Expanding this from 1963, the RAF offered university scholarships to those applicants for GD or Technical branches (later also the Equipment, Supply and Education branches) who had already secured university admission. Logically, in 1968, the RAF declared that all officers for permanent commission would in future be university educated. Graduates would attend Cranwell after their studies for one year of officer training and professional or flying training. Consequently, having entered Cranwell in 1970, the last entry of non-graduate flight cadets passed out in 1973.

Boy entrants, training to be air radar mechanics, receive instruction on an AI.17 radar array of a Javelin at No. 2 School of Technical Training, RAF Cosford, on 4 November 1959. The training of RAF personnel was the responsibility of Flying Training Command and Technical Training Command. The former oversaw the training of aircrew via the Flying Training Schools, the Air Navigation Schools, and the RAF College Cranwell. It was also responsible for post-entry training at Operational Conversion Units, the College of Air Warfare and the Central Flying School. Technical Training Command was responsible for training all other trades and branches via RAF Technical College Henlow, the various schools of technical, radio or administrative training and the RAF Regiment Depot at Catterick. In 1968, as part of a defence review, the two commands merged to form a single RAF Training Command. *(RAF-T 1310)*

Senior Flight Cadets Mike Porter and Chris Green, and Under Officer Peter Symes of No. 76 Entry, destined for the Equipment and Secretarial branches, standing on the 'Orange' outside the Royal Air Force College Cranwell, summer 1959. The Junior Entries, the two most recent entries, lived under a challenging regime characterized initially by drill and 'bull'. Air Chief Marshal Sir Richard Johns of No. 76 Entry: *'Cranwell was tough; certainly the first couple of terms were very tough ... I don't think you could have conditions like that now. There was a form of institutionalized bullying by the Entry above called crowing, and the parade square was very much the centre of your life, certainly for the first three months ... what they were doing was forming you into an entry.'* Initially housed in barrack rooms within First World War brick huts, after the first term cadets moved into private bedsits within a separate block, later moving into the College building. *(RAF-T 1088)*

Senior flight cadets give a presentation on the 1943 invasion of Sicily to fellow cadets and a tri-service panel of tutors as part of their studies at the RAF College, April 1962. In addition to flying or professional training, the three (at times two and a half) year syllabus at Cranwell provided cadets with an education similar to a university degree. The first year provided all cadets, regardless of social background, with a similar academic footing before embarking on more advanced teaching in the second and third years. In 1959, the syllabus was changed to enable cadets to specialize either in science or arts subjects, each stream having an equivalent civilian qualification. All cadets were required to undertake an element in Military Studies, learning about the history and conduct of war and international affairs. *(RAF-T 3078)*

Provost T.1 WV429 of No. 6 Flying Training School (6 FTS), RAF Ternhill, Shropshire, flies alongside Vampire T.11 XD520 of 5 FTS, RAF Oakington. The Provost-Vampire combination formed a new flying training sequence for RAF pilots. The sixty-week course consisted of 120 hours of basic flying training on the Provost and 110 hours of advanced flying to 'wings standard' on the Vampire. Previously pilots graduated on piston aircraft following sixteen weeks on the Percival Prentice and thirty-two on the Boulton Paul Balliol. A further jet training stage of up to eighteen weeks on the Meteor or Vampire then followed. Introducing trainees to an easy to handle jet aircraft in training prevented the need for the additional jet stage, considerably shortening the course. The first trainees to use a new Provost-Vampire flying training sequence graduated from RAF Oakington on 9 June 1954. (RAF-T 10)

Flying instructors, Flight Lieutenants Bob Newell and John Davis, plan a flight with Senior Under Officer Martin Freeman and Flight Cadet Tom Porteous, in front of Vampire T.11s of the RAF College's Flying Wing, on 23 June 1959. The college's distinctive markings, bands of Cambridge blue edged with Oxford blue, can be seen on the aircraft's fuselages, as can the yellow bands indicating Flying Training Command. In 1956, after its runways were lengthened to allow jet flying, Cranwell adopted the Provost-Vampire training sequence. For the first time cadets completed their jet flying training at the college. All first year cadets undertook air experience on the de Havilland Chipmunk, and sixty hours' basic navigation training on the Boston Marathon or Vickers Valetta. In the second year they commenced basic flying training on the Provost. In 1959, the training syllabus changed once again when Jet Provosts were introduced as the college's principal flying training aircraft. *(RAF-T 1110)*

A flight cadet at the RAF College Cranwell receives guidance from his flying instructor while seated in a Jet Provost T.3, c. 1964. In 1955, 2 FTS at RAF Hullavington trialled the Jet Provost T.1 as a basic jet trainer in place of the piston Provost. Proving popular with its student / instructor side-by-side cockpit and easy handling characteristics, from 1959, the Jet Provost T.3 became the RAF's standard basic trainer in a shorter all-jet training sequence. In 1959, when it received the Jet Provost, the RAF College abandoned advanced flying training. Flight cadets would be trained to 'wings standard' on Jet Provosts, before progressing after graduation to the Vampire (later Gnat) stage at 4 FTS at RAF Valley or 5 FTS at RAF Oakington. The Jet Provost remained the RAF's principal basic trainer until 1993. (RAF-T 5452)

Twelve Folland Gnat T.1s with flying instructors of 4 FTS seen at a press day in October 1963, to mark the aircraft's introduction to service the previous year. By the early 1960s, the antiquated Vampire T.11 was no longer sufficient to train pilots destined to fly the Lightning. Replacing the Vampire, the transonic Gnat provided pilots with the required fast jet experience prior to operating the Lightning. After 170 hours of basic training on Jet Provosts, newly qualified pilots undertook seventy hours of advanced training on Gnats. The first Gnats were delivered to the Central Flying School at RAF Little Rissington in February 1962 and to RAF Valley in November that year. The final Gnat class graduated at RAF Valley on 24 November 1978. Note the bright orange paint of Flying Training Command replacing the earlier yellow bands. Found to fade quickly, the new scheme was soon replaced by orange vinyl strips. *(RAF-T 3630)*

Navigator cadets under training in a Vickers Valetta T.3 'flying classroom' of No. 2 Air Navigation School at RAF Thorney Island, 29 May 1959. Note the astral domes for use with the Mark 9 Sextant during day and night training. By 1957, after graduating from the Initial Training School at South Cerney, Direct Entry navigator cadets passed to 2 ANS at RAF Thorney Island for a forty-nine week course of 100 hours' basic air navigation and a further 100 hours of advanced training, using the Valetta and Varsity. In 1962, 2 ANS moved to RAF Hullavington and abandoned 'all through' training. No. 2 ANS continued to provide basic navigation training on Varsity and Valetta aircraft during an eight-month course, while 1 ANS provided a further four-month advanced course using the Varsity and the Meteor NF(T)14 at RAF Stradishall. In 1965, 2 ANS moved to RAF Gaydon, while at 1 ANS the Meteors were replaced as the advanced trainer by the Hawker Siddeley Dominie. *(RAF-T 672)*

Lightning T.4 XM997 of 226 OCU is seen 'beating up' the airfield at RAF Coltishall to mark the unit's move there in April 1964. The aircraft is wearing the colours of 145 Squadron, the OCU's alternative 'shadow' designation. Operational Conversion Units provided training to pilots being posted to operational squadrons with unfamiliar aircraft. Due to the aircraft's characteristics, pilots destined for Lightning squadrons were expected to have first completed an operational tour on Hunters or Javelins. By 1964, this was no longer practical and pilots went to 226 OCU via additional training on the Hunter, usually at 229 OCU at RAF Chivernor. The first three pilots posted to Lightning squadrons as 'first tourists' left Coltishall in October 1964. No. 226 OCU was formed in June 1963 from the Lightning Conversion Squadron at RAF Middleton St George. It remained at Coltishall until September 1974 when it disbanded, reequipping with Jaguars. *(RAF-T 4920)*

Technical cadets are instructed on a Rolls-Royce Avon jet engine by a warrant officer instructor at RAF Technical College Henlow, c. 1960. The Technical College provided officer training, basic studies and professional training for cadets seeking permanent commission in the Technical branch as mechanical or electrical engineers. The college also provided regular training and post-graduate studies in the branch's sub-divisions of armament, engineering and signals. From 1949, there were two types of Technical Cadetship; Henlow cadetships took place over four years at the college, while university cadets started with twelve months at Henlow followed by a three-year degree course at a university. In 1965, the RAF Technical College closed and the technical training role was absorbed by the new Department of Engineering at Cranwell. The Technical branch was renamed the Engineering branch in 1966. *(RAF-T 1293)*

Candidates seeking a commission in the Women's Royal Air Force undertake a teamwork selection exercise at the Ground Officers' Selection Centre, RAF Biggin Hill, in November 1960. The Ground Officers' Selection Centre, initially at RAF Uxbridge but from 1959 at RAF Biggin Hill, was responsible for the selection, by means of medical, educational and aptitude tests, of candidates for commissioning into the RAF ground branches and the WRAF. Selection for the General Duties (flying) branch was made at the Aircrew Selection Centre at RAF Hornchurch. In 1962, the Aircrew Selection Centre also moved to Biggin Hill and with the GOSC formed the Officers' and Aircrew Selection Centre, selecting all candidates for commissioning into the RAF and WRAF. *(RAF-T 2285)*

Three men, with suitcases in hand, receive instructions from a master signaller after arriving for a commissioning course at the Officer Cadet Training Unit (OCTU) at RAF Feltwell in 1964. The OCTU, which until the previous year had been based at RAF Jurby, Isle of Man, provided the training for over 60 per cent of new officers entering the RAF, university entrants, entrants to the ground branches (except technical cadets) including WRAF officers, and existing service personnel selected for commission. The commissioning course usually lasted just sixteen weeks, with a new course starting each month. Shorter one-month courses were held for officers re-entering the service and for medical officers or chaplains. WRAF candidates were initially trained at the WRAF OCTU at RAF Hawkinge, but in 1962 this merged with the OCTU at Jurby. The OCTU remained at Feltwell until 1966 when it moved to RAF Henlow. *(RAF-T 5767)*

WRAF recruits receive instruction from a corporal drill instructor during their first week of recruit training at the WRAF Depot at RAF Spitalgate in 1965. On joining the service WRAF recruits undertook eight weeks of basic training at Spitalgate. Prior to 1960, this was provided at the WRAF School of Recruit Training at RAF Wilmslow. WRAF recruitment emphasized the vital part women were playing in the Cold War. The WRAF Director in 1950, Air Commandant Nancy Salmon: '[the WRAF was] sharing fully in the task of maintaining a strong and efficient Service – and thus, in a wider sphere, making their own contribution towards the preservation of world peace.' Between 1958 and 1961, the WRAF offered Local Service engagements, which allowed women to join and, after three weeks' of basic training at RAF Hawkinge, work at a local station and return to the family home in the evening. (RAF-T 4980)

Cadets playing rugby at the RAF Technical College Henlow, on 28 October 1959. Sport and recreation were an important part of recruit and cadet training. Air Marshal Sir John Whitworth Jones, AOC Technical Training Command, in 1950: *'Modern methods of recruit training are designed to form the man in a balanced manner, giving proper weight to his physical, mental and spiritual development.'* Obligatory sport sessions including football, rugby and cross-country running were built into the training programme. Activities such as gliding, sailing, potholing and horse riding, not available in recruits' civilian lives, were also available. Often, less athletically minded recruits were given permission to leave camp, ostensibly to participate in activities such as golf or cycling, but instead recruits spent the time in local cafes. Throughout the RAF, Wednesday afternoons were traditionally set aside for sports. Accomplished sportsmen were encouraged and enabled to represent their squadron, station or command. *(RAF-T 1309)*

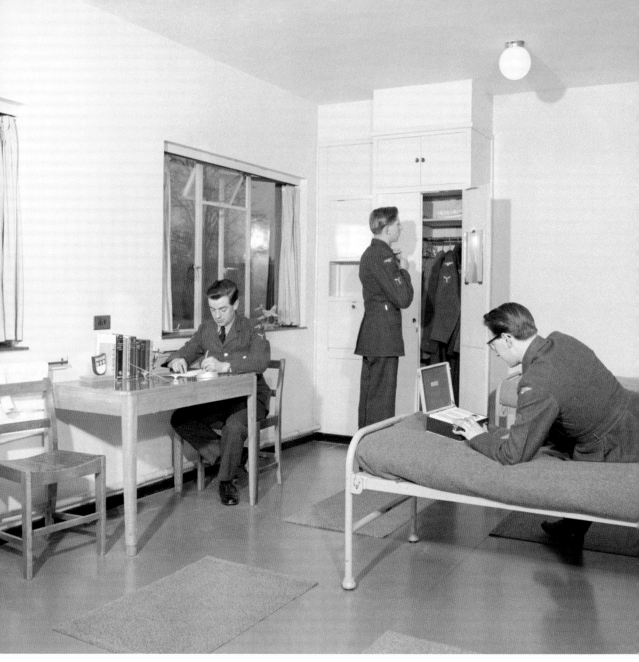

A room in a new accommodation block for single airmen built at RAF Medmenham in February 1957. During the 1950s, the limited availability and poor standard of RAF accommodation was considered a significant deterrent to recruitment. Consequently, throughout the 1950s and 1960s a massive building programme was undertaken to replace the many often temporary accommodation buildings constructed before the Second World War. Replacing the prefab Nissen-style huts were new two or three storey brick-built barracks consisting of centrally heated rooms, each holding four to six airmen or airwomen. Though the RAF often promoted these new buildings in recruitment brochures as the standard, new recruits at the Schools of Recruit Training and boy entrants and apprentices in the Initial Training Squadrons were still being accommodated in the old huts well into the 1960s. Once basic training was completed, recruits moved into more permanent, better quality accommodation. *(RAF-T 797)*

A flight lieutenant and his family outside their married quarter at RAF Cranwell, in 1967. In 1945, there were only 6,000 RAF married quarters available for personnel in the UK; by 1956 there were 21,000 with another 5,000 under construction. More were built in the 1960s to accommodate service families brought back from stations in the Middle East and Far East. From a 1966 recruitment brochure: *'Demand for married quarters exceeds supply … Rents are reasonable and they are furnished throughout. Accommodation in one of the newly designed houses consists of living and dining room, well fitted kitchen, [two or three] bedrooms, bathroom etc. and an outside storage room. Altogether the modern married quarters in the Royal Air Force satisfy the highest standards of design, construction and decoration.'* Quarters for officers often differed to airmen's by having better quality furniture, a front garden and a garage with a drive. *(RAF-T 7214)*

Boy entrants, training to be armament mechanics, attach a practice 1,000lb bomb to a Hawker Hunter instructional airframe at No. 4 School of Technical Training (SoTT), RAF St Athan, 28 October 1959. Each year 1,000 new boy entrants would sign-up. By January 1960, they were being trained at three Schools of Technical Training. The busiest of these, No. 2 SoTT at RAF Cosford, trained boys to be air and ground wireless mechanics, air radar mechanics, telegraphists, and photographers. Clerks, cooks, stewards and suppliers attended No. 3 SoTT at RAF Hereford. As well as armament mechanics, No. 4 SoTT trained airframe, engine and instruments mechanics, and air and ground electricians. Teaching was split equally between theoretical instruction and practical experience, with weekly classroom tests and end of term examinations to ensure progress. *(RAF-T 1328)*

Boy entrants, training to be photographers at No. 2 School of Technical Training, RAF Cosford, learn to use a light meter while photographing the radar array of a Vampire NF.10, November 1959. Boy entrants and apprentices were admitted in January, May and September each year, with each intake forming an Entry. After three months in the Initial Training Squadron, boys were placed in training squadrons, based on their chosen trade. Both boy entrants and apprentices wore the standard RAF 'other ranks' uniform but with insignia consisting of a colour backed badge in the shape of an encircled propeller and a coloured, or in the case of boy entrants chequered, band on the service dress hat. The colour of hatband and badge indicated establishment, wing and squadron. The 'blood and custard' hat band and yellow badge in the photograph shows the photographers were in 1 Squadron, 1 Wing at RAF Cosford. *(RAF-T 1199)*

Leading Aircraft Apprentice Jim Stott and Corporal Aircraft Apprentice Dave Purser are seen talking with a flight lieutenant at RAF Halton in November 1964. Dave Purser was Pipe Major in 2 Wing's volunteer Apprentice Band, as denoted by the insignia and inverted chevrons on his lower left sleeve. Apprentices were largely subject to the same service regulations as adult entrants. Apprentice NCOs aided station officers and NCOs in administering military discipline, often enthusiastically and sometimes extra-judiciously, often in the form of regular kit inspections. Leading apprentices were in charge of a room of twenty boys; corporal apprentices a landing of two barrack rooms; sergeant apprentices a block of one hundred boys. Flight sergeant apprentices were in charge of an entire Apprentice Wing. In return, apprentice NCOs were entitled to additional privileges; for example they had their own rooms within the block for which they were in charge and were issued with additional leave passes. *(RAF-T 4789)*

Administrative apprentices (pay accountants) under training at RAF Bircham Newton, 24 July 1959. By the mid-1950s, the apprentice schools were at three principal sites. Administrative apprentices were trained to be clerks, pay accountants and suppliers at the Administrative Apprentice Training School at RAF Hereford. Between January 1959 and January 1963, the school briefly relocated to Bircham Newton. Aircraft apprentices were trained at No. 1 School of Technical Training at RAF Halton to be Fitters on engines, airframes and instruments. Apprentices destined for the Air and Ground Radio trades were taught at No. 1 Radio School at RAF Locking. The three-year training led apprentices to be trained to higher level than boy entrants. Each year, outstanding administrative apprentices were offered Cranwell cadetships to obtain commissions in the Secretarial or General Duties branches. Similarly, aircraft apprentices could also be offered cadetships for the Technical branch at Henlow or General Duties branch at Cranwell. *(RAF-T 1152)*

Aircraft apprentices of the 91st Entry at No. 1 School of Technical Training, RAF Halton, receiving 'Final Airframes' training from instructor Mr Maynall in a classroom hangar containing Hunter instructional airframes in July 1959. David Branchett, an aircraft apprentice (propulsion) in 90th Entry at Halton from September 1958, describes a routine similar to grammar school: 'It consisted of a five and a half day week, Wednesday afternoons were for sport, Saturdays mornings for barrack inspections, wing parades or PT. Reveille was at 0645, breakfast, tidy barrack then outside to march down behind the Wing pipe band to either workshops or schools. Normally each day would be spent split between these two centres of learning. Lunchtime we were marched back up the hill and down again an hour later for afternoon sessions until teatime, when we were marched back up again.' (RAF-T 1136)

Flight Lieutenant George Thorn instructs new recruits at the RAF School of Catering at RAF Hereford in June 1962. The RAF School of Catering, originally at RAF Halton, was the training establishment for chefs and stewards in the Catering trade group. In September 1958, it moved from RAF Halton to RAF Hereford where, in 1959, it merged with the School of Cookery, which had moved from RAF Cosford. By 1960, the new School of Catering was responsible for providing trade training for all recruits to the RAF and WRAF catering trade group, including officers of the catering branch, apprentices and, until 1965, boy entrants. Training was also provided to air quartermasters and nursing staff. Hereford remained the seat of learning for all recruits, officers and apprentices destined for the Catering branch or trade until the 1980s. *(RAF-T 3348)*

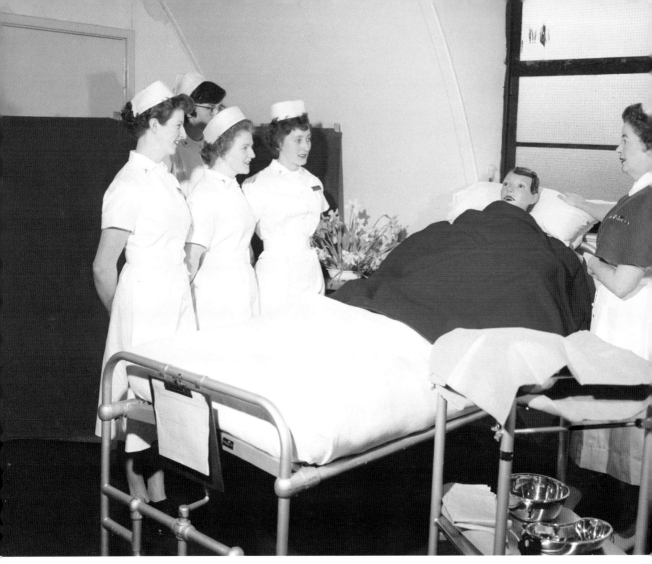

A squadron officer of the Princess Mary's Royal Air Force Nursing Service, uses a dummy to instruct nurses undergoing training at the RAF Hospital Ely, 18 January 1961. Although holding a WRAF rank, nursing staff were usually referred to by their professional titles; squadron officer was equivalent to matron. Initially containing only commissioned personnel, in 1956 'other ranks' nursing assistants from the WRAF were transferred to the PMRAFNS. The PMRAFNS provided nursing care to service personnel and their families within the RAF's hospitals and station sick quarters in the UK and around the globe. RAFH Ely was one of three hospitals in the United Kingdom providing nursing training; the others were Halton and Wroughton. Also providing medical care to personnel were the RAF Medical branch, which supplied the RAF's medical officers while the Medical trade group provided the mostly non-commissioned, male nursing attendants. Nursing attendants, regulars and boy entrants, were trained at No. 2 School of Technical Training RAF Cosford. *(RAF-T 2442)*

Recruits, training to be firemen, practise aircraft crash rescue techniques during trade training at the Fire Training School, RAF Catterick, on 9 April 1962. In the background is a Thorneycroft Dual Purpose Mark I crash tender. In late 1955, the role of RAF fireman was transferred to the RAF Regiment trade group. Consequently, in July 1959 the training of the now 'RAF Regiment firemen' and 'fire officers', was transferred from the RAF School of Firefighting and Rescue at RAF Sutton on Hull to the Fire Fighting and Special Safety Squadron (later called the Fire Fighting and Rescue Training Squadron) at the RAF Regiment's Depot at RAF Catterick. Having passed recruit training, new recruits were posted to Catterick for an nine-week trade training course. Trade training consisted of an element in the use of vehicles and equipment for crash rescue, aircraft firefighting and domestic firefighting. *(RAF-T 3109)*

Chapter Six

Aerobatic Display Teams

Display flying has existed since the early days of flight, but a single official RAF aerobatic team is a more recent concept. After the Second World War, temporary and unofficial teams were formed by front-line units wishing to display the skill of their pilots in their increasingly advanced aircraft. By their heyday in the late-1950s, these teams had become world famous for their innovative and daring displays. The RAF quickly recognized the benefit of these teams for public relations and recruitment, creating the first official teams to represent the force at the many displays held each year. Due to the budget concerns of the early 1960s, the majority of teams disbanded and by 1965 the Red Arrows had formed, becoming the only official RAF aerobatic team.

RAF open days, which between the wars had included a popular flying program, restarted after the Second World War. Timed to coincide with the Battle of Britain anniversary, each September the RAF opened to the public a growing number of air stations across the country. At these RAF 'At Home' days, visitors were presented with static displays of front-line aircraft, which from the first open day in 1945, included jet-engine Meteors and Vampires alongside the wartime Spitfires, Hurricanes and Mosquitos. During the flying programme slow, pre-war aircraft performed low-level aerobatics while wartime fighters recreated the familiar sights and sounds of dogfights. Participating jet aircraft were initially restricted to providing solo displays or team flypasts.

During the summer of 1947, three Vampires from 54 Squadron performed formation aerobatic routines at a number of air galas in Britain and Europe. This team was the RAF's first jet aerobatic display team and following its success and the public's awed reaction, further squadron teams of Vampires and Meteors were formed soon after.

Assembled by front-line units, teams were considered to be beneficial not only for public relations but also seen as having a positive effect on squadron operations, and were not actively discouraged by Fighter Command. Competition between pilots to join a team was fierce, with only the best achieving a place. Many additional hours were spent flying in order to qualify for a position. In training for each season, team members perfected close formation flying, an element heavily used in operational flying. With so many squadrons assembling teams, competition between them to represent Fighter Command at an event was intense.

By 1952, just five years after the first team performed, there were thirty-five Meteor or Vampire equipped teams representing units of Fighter Command, 2TAF, Royal Auxiliary Air Force and Flying Training Command. Immediately following the introduction of the Sabre in late-1953, four teams were assembled to participate in the 1954 season. As faster more powerful aircraft entered squadron service, teams were quickly formed to show off their capabilities to the watching public.

Soon after arriving in squadron service in 1954, the Hunter was recognized as an impressive aircraft. The later models, particularly the Hunter F.6 with its more powerful engine and improved flying controls, proved a successful display aircraft and proved very popular with both pilot and spectator. For the next fifteen years teams of Hunters were the highlight on the display circuit. In 1955, the Hunter's first display season, four such teams performed, including a new team from 54 Squadron called The Black Knights and 43 Squadron's The Fighting Cocks. By 1957, there were no fewer than eleven Hunter teams from Fighter Command, 2TAF or Flying Training Command.

By the mid-1950s, faced with a growing number of displays each year requiring time to train and participate, squadrons found performing whilst maintaining operational status increasingly difficult. This led Fighter Command to select an official team to represent it at the principal shows. While 'unofficial' teams continued to display, the burden of performing was significantly reduced. The first official team, The Black Knights, performed at twenty-one shows during the 1955 season. In 1956, two excellent Hunter teams were nominated to share official status. The Fighting Cocks based at RAF Leuchars in Fife represented 13 Group covering Scotland and the north of England, while 111 Squadron at RAF North Weald in Essex represented 11 Group in the south, prompting fiercely competitive displays by the two teams. From 1957, 111 Squadron's team, by now called The Black Arrows following a repaint in gloss black, emerged as the dominant team representing Fighter Command for four years until 1960. During that time, the team became world-renowned, largely thanks to the innovative displays of team leaders Squadron Leaders Roger Topp and later Peter Latham. Presented with the unenviable task of following The Black Arrows in 1961, 92 Squadron's The Blue Diamonds became the last of the official teams flying the Hunter, though squadrons equipped with the aircraft continued to form teams until 1969. As so many Hunter teams had before them, The Black Arrows and The Blue Diamonds were both disbanded in 1962 as their squadrons re-equipped with the Lightning.

In 1960, soon after receiving the RAF's first four operational Lightnings, 74 Squadron formed The Tigers. In 1962, after performing 'unofficially' for two years, The Tigers succeeded The Blue Diamonds, becoming Fighter Command's first official Lightning team. The Tigers were followed the following year by a nine ship team, The Firebirds of 56 Squadron. Despite the RAF's apparent enthusiasm to display the impressive Lightning with its speed, power and noise, it was not a suitable aircraft for the refined movements of aerobatic display. Only three Lightning teams were formed between 1960 and 1965, from 74 and 56 Squadrons and also 111 Squadron's new team, The Black Diamonds.

By 1963, it had become apparent that with the reduction in the number of squadrons and aircraft within Fighter Command since 1957, few squadrons were able to provide enough men and machines to regularly perform. Maintaining a team each year took one of the five Lightning squadrons out of the front line, at a time when the RAF was seeing an increase in air defence operations. The Firebirds of 1963 was to be the last team provided by an operational squadron.

Establishments of Flying Training Command, such as the Central Flying School, RAF College Cranwell and the Flying Training Schools, had often assembled informal teams to allow flying instructors a way to develop their own flying skills. From the late 1940s, the Prentice, Chipmunk and Provost trainers used by these teams were gradually replaced with Meteors,

Vampires and later Jet Provosts. By the early 1960s, these establishments were fully equipped with jets, and the responsibility of providing the RAF's official team passed from Fighter Command to Flying Training Command.

In 1964, the RAF selected its first official team from the command; the Jet Provost equipped Red Pelicans of Central Flying School at RAF Little Rissington. Although skilfully piloted, the underpowered Jet Provost was a disappointing display aircraft and the routines considered mundane compared with the Lightning and Hunter that had preceded it. In 1962 No. 4 Flying Training School at RAF Valley began training with the Gnat. Two years later one of 4FTS's Qualified Flying Instructors, Flight Lieutenant Lee Jones, previously a pilot with The Black Arrows, recognized the display potential of this aircraft and formed The Yellowjacks. Though the team wasn't the nominated team for 1964, it was a very popular attraction wherever it performed, often alongside the official Red Pelicans. Lasting just one season, The Yellowjacks disbanded in October 1964.

In March 1965, Jones was posted to the Central Flying School at RAF Little Rissington. At CFS he was asked to lead another Gnat team. Having adopted CFS's red paint scheme, the team was named The Red Arrows, in homage to The Black Arrows. The Red Arrows' first public performance was in May 1965 at the RAF Biggin Hill International Air Fair. By the end of their first year they had completed fifty displays. For the first time all the pilots, who were drawn from the instructing staff at CFS, had no other responsibilities but to train with the team to perfect the displays. The Red Arrows' initial years were full of concerns about affordability, with teams varying in size due to availability of aircraft. However, in recognition of the team's benefit to RAF public relations following its successful display season during the RAF's 50th anniversary year in 1968, the following year The Red Arrows was designated as the permanent official Royal Air Force Aerobatic Team.

Despite the RAF, since 1955, nominating teams to represent it, others continued to display. In 1955 there were no fewer than thirty-seven teams formed by units from Fighter Command, 2TAF and Flying Training Command, even two Canberra teams from Bomber Command. Some 'unofficial' teams such as Cranwell's Lincolnshire Poachers and 1 FTS's Gin Formation gained enthusiastic followers. The various defence cuts of the 1950s and 1960s reduced the number of teams to fewer than twenty by the time The Red Arrows formed in 1965. In 1969, a team from 2 Squadron, RAF Germany, the last Hunter team and the last drawn from a front-line squadron, disbanded leaving just eight teams from Training Command. The oil crises of the early 1970s further reduced the number of teams over the next few years and by 1990, The Red Arrows was the sole remaining RAF aerobatic display team.

Four Hunter F.4s, WV324, WV366, WV387 and XF299, of 43 Squadron's The Fighting Cocks, are seen rehearsing on 13 June 1956 for the Farnborough Air Show. The Fighting Cocks was established in March 1955 by Squadron Leader Roy le Long. Later that year the team, now led by Flight Lieutenant Peter Bairstow, was enlarged from three to four aircraft so as to increase the variety of formations and display elements available to them. One of the first Hunter teams, The Fighting Cocks was also one of the first to achieve an international reputation for excellence. The team performing at Farnborough with Bairstow comprised Flying Officers Ron Smith, Mike Stabler and Marcus Wild. *(RAF-T 9)*

RAF College Cranwell's first jet display team consisting of four Vampire FB.9s WR146, WR209, WR242, WR247 seen here in 1956, flown by Flight Lieutenant Bidie leading Flight Lieutenant Warren and Flying Officers Durrant and Penrose. This unnamed team was disbanded in 1961. In 1956, units of Flying Training Command operated no fewer than ten teams of Vampires and Meteors. These included two teams of Vampires at 5 FTS at RAF Oakington, with another at 8 FTS at RAF Swinderby and a team of Meteors at both the RAF Flying College at RAF Strubby and the Central Flying School at RAF Little Rissington. Initially replaced by newer aircraft, increasingly display teams reverted to older aircraft for their displays with CFS continuing to operate the vintage pair of a Meteor and Vampire until 1988. *(RAF-T 34)*

Ground crew defuel two of The Black Arrows' Hunter F.6s at RAF North Weald, c. 1957. No 111 Squadron's Hunter display team was formed in June 1955 by the squadron's commanding officer, Squadron Leader Roger Topp. Initially performing with four aircraft, in 1956 it increased to five. When, in the following year, it became an official RAF team it adopted a distinctive black paint scheme, leading to the acceptance of the name The Black Arrows. Such was the team's success, it remained the RAF's official team until 1960, being led by Squadron Leader Peter Latham from 1959. On the left of the image is XG194, the aircraft flown by Topp during the 1958 world record formation loop. (RAF-T 232)

A five-ship formation by The Black Arrows, during the 1957 display season. While most teams in the 1957 season flew with four or five aircraft, The Black Arrows, seen here, started with five but quickly increased to seven and then nine. Topp pushed the boundaries of formation flying, constantly reworking the team's routines. In September 1958, he led several sixteen aircraft displays, and achieved a world record twenty-two aircraft mass formation loop at the Society of British Aircraft Constructors air show at Farnborough. *Flight* magazine: '*Rearing up they disclose themselves in three impeccable chevrons of seven and continue up and over to complete the most wonderful mass aerobatic manoeuvre ever seen at Farnborough.*' During its time as Fighter Command's nominated team, The Black Arrows became the world's premier display team thanks to Topp and Latham's experimentation with new formations. *(RAF-T 240)*

Squadron Leader Roger Topp and other pilots from The Black Arrows sign autographs for excited schoolboys at the 1958 Schoolboys Own Exhibition at Olympia, London. So popular were the many display teams during the 1950s, the pilots, particularly of The Black Arrows, were household names, becoming heroes to children and adults alike. Aerobatic display teams were found to be an excellent public relations tool. The RAF recognized this and was keen to exploit the popularity of the teams to encourage schoolboys dreaming of becoming the next generation of pilots. (RAF-T 534)

At RAF Middleton St George in 1961, 92 Squadron's The Blue Diamonds pose for a formal photograph with their Hunter F.6s upon becoming the RAF's official display team. Selected to replace The Black Arrows, the pilots of The Blue Diamonds led by Squadron Leader Brian Mercer, a former Black Arrows pilot, wanted to better the standard of their predecessor. Formed as a team of nine aircraft it increased on occasion to twelve or sixteen and developed a range of new formations including its trademark 'Diamond Sixteen' formation. Mercer has subsequently remarked that he wanted to emerge from the influence of 111 Squadron, but never did: '*The real issue here was the nostalgia for the Black Arrows who had been first and were in the display business for longer than us and we simply could not get out of their shadow.*' The team disbanded at the end of 1962. (RAF-T 2527)

Five of The Blue Diamonds' Hunter F.6s in tight line abreast formation. One way The Blue Diamonds attempted to distinguish itself from its predecessor was the team colour applied during 1961 pre-season training. The paint scheme of a royal blue colour with a white lightning flash and squadron decals on the nose, was chosen by Mercer specifically: *'Treble One was black. White gets oil-stained beneath the fuselage. Red is the Belgian team's colour. Orange is an aesthetic disaster. Yellow is for Training Command. Green is considered unlucky. But blue is the RAF colour.'* Later that year, derived from a comment in a German newspaper after a performance at RAF Wildenrath, the team adopted the name The Blue Diamonds. *(RAF-T 2528)*

The Firebirds of 56 Squadron from RAF Wattisham, led by Squadron Leader Dave Seward, seen here practising their signature 'Diamond Nine' formation roll in 1963. After receiving the Lightning F.1A in 1961, a team of nine aircraft was formed. As was becoming convention for teams, it adopted a distinct colour scheme, in this case the tail and wing leading edges were painted scarlet. In 1963, by now called The Firebirds after the squadron emblem, it was selected to replace 74 Squadron's The Tigers as the official team. The RAF was increasingly concerned that displaying The Firebirds withdrew a front-line squadron from the order of battle. No. 56 Squadron was the last Fighter Command squadron to provide an official team. (RAF-T 4163)

The Black Dragons from 234(R) Squadron, part of 229 OCU, line up in front of a Hunter F.6 at RAF Chivenor in 1963. Formed by Lee Jones in 1958, The Black Dragons was one of the few high-profile teams operated by an Operational Conversion Unit. With the disbandment in 1962 of The Black Arrows and The Blue Diamonds, The Black Dragons became the only UK-based Hunter team. In 1963, although The Firebirds was the RAF's premier team, The Black Dragons assumed the role of representative Hunter team. It disbanded at the end of that year. The pilots are from left to right: H. A. Tony Park, R. V. A. 'Porky' Munro, Ron Wood, Ernie Powell and Fred A. Trowern. *(RAF-T 5032)*

The unimaginatively named CFS Jet Aerobatic Team, seen here practising in 1958, was one of several successful jet display teams to emerge from the Central Flying School after the Second World War. In 1952, the Meteorites, a team of four Meteor T.7s, was formed. It was later renamed The Pelicans after the school's mascot. In 1958, equipped with the new Jet Provost T.1 trainer, CFS Jet Aerobatic Team was formed led by Flight Lieutenant Norman Giffin. The team was famed for its inverted leader formation in which Giffin flew ahead of the formation in an inverted position. Giffin also designed the distinctive red and white paint scheme. The team disbanded after just one year to be replaced by a synchronized pair called The Redskins during the 1959 season. *(RAF-T 575)*

Seen here led by Flight Lieutenant Terry Lloyd in 1964 are Jet Provost T.4s of the Central Flying School's The Red Pelicans, Flying Training Command's first official display team. Following the success of the 1958 CFS Jet Aerobatic Team using the Jet Provost T.1, a second team with four T.3s was assembled in 1960. In 1962, this was replaced by a larger team of five T.4s and named The Red Pelicans having adopted CFS's bright red colour scheme and emblem. The team was increased to six aircraft for the 1963 season. On the introduction at CFS of the Red Arrows as the permanent official team, The Red Pelicans was reduced to four aircraft and repainted in red and white. The team was finally disbanded in 1973 during the Middle East fuel crisis. *(RAF-T 4736)*

Three Jet Provost T.4s of the RAF College Cranwell's 'The Poachers', led by Squadron Leader Iain Panton, are seen climbing into an inverted loop for a publicity photograph in the summer of 1964. The photographer is probably flying in the team's fourth aircraft. After assembling several informal Provost teams since 1961, in 1963, a four-ship team called The Poachers, led by Squadron Leader Panton was founded as the RAF College's display team, in place of the previous Vampire team. The Poachers principally performed at the College or other RAF establishments. In 1968, in line with the rest of Training Command teams, the team adopted a red and white paint scheme. *(RAF-T 4422)*

Five Folland Gnat T.1s from 4 FTS, RAF Valley, practise an inverted loop in 'T' formation, over Holyhead in 1964. Introduced to the RAF in 1962, against expectations the Gnat was found to be an excellent aerobatics aircraft. Flight Lieutenant Lee Jones: *'The Gnat was delightful but sensitive, and much more difficult for formation aerobatics than the Hunter – on the other hand by using 10 degrees flap and dropping the slipper tanks we had a perfect display aircraft. It "looked" so fast and could be pulled in to stay close to crowd centre while never exceeding 300–310 knots.'* To be distinctive from other teams, the aircraft were painted in the yellow colour scheme of Flying Training Command, becoming known as The Yellowjacks. It only performed during the 1964 season before being disbanded. *(RAF-T 4715)*

Pilots of The Yellowjacks listen to a briefing by team founder Lee Jones at RAF Valley during their only season in 1964. Seated left to right, they are: Ray Hoggarth (reserve pilot), Derrick McSweeney, Henry Prince (reserve pilot), Peter Hay, Gerry Ranscombe and Guy Whitley. Lee Jones was a significant player in the world of British aerobatic flying. As well as establishing The YellowJacks, he had previously led the Black Dragons of 229 OCU during 1958–1959, as well as being a member of the final Black Arrows team in 1960. After The Yellowjacks disbanded, Jones moved to the Central Flying School where he established The Red Arrows, along with Ranscombe, Hay and Prince. *(RAF-T 4725)*

The nine pilots of The Red Arrows of 1966 with ground support crew at RAF Fairford. The pilots are in order of position in the team (from left to right): Ray Hanna (Red Leader), Derek Bell, Bill Langworthy, Pete Evans, Roy Booth, Henry Prince, Tim Nelson, Frank Hoare and Doug McGregor. In 1969, with the growing public profile of the team, it received the status of a distinct unit, with air and ground crew appointed directly to the team, exclusive of other duties. Although a Central Flying School team, they were based away from Little Rissington, initially at RAF Fairford, but later at RAF Kemble. *(RAF-T 6283)*

The seven Gnats of The Red Arrows flying in 'King's Cross' formation in 1966, near their base at RAF Kemble. The number of Gnats available during their first season limited the team to seven aircraft. In 1966, with the unit up to strength, new leader Ray Hanna was occasionally granted permission to perform with nine aircraft. Though he wished to continue performing with nine, financial cuts to the RAF once again meant limited available aircraft, and the 1967 team returned to just seven aircraft. In 1968, however, The Red Arrows was firmly established as a nine aircraft team. Barring technical failure or accident, the team has performed with nine since. *(RAF-T 6299)*

The newly established nine aircraft Red Arrows team of 1969 is seen flying in line abreast formation. The aircraft are wearing the new paint scheme that evolved between the 1966 and 1969 seasons, including a full red, white and blue tail fin added after the 1967 season and a white lightning flash forward of the engine air intake, suggested by Hanna and added at the end of the 1968 season. Establishing The Red Arrows as an independent unit allowed the pilots time to practise and perform, without the distraction of training duties. This dramatically improved the routines and performances and increased the number of displays that could be performed. *(RAF-T 8168)*

A stunning image of The Red Arrows, seen climbing whilst in their signature 'Diamond Nine' formation and trailing smoke, one of a series of photographs taken to promote the RAF during its 50th anniversary in 1968. That year was a very busy year, with the team undertaking no fewer than ninety-eight displays, promoting the RAF and Britain at home and overseas. Under Ray Hanna, The Red Arrows, more than any of its contemporary teams, developed a way of flying that provided spectators with a continuous, uninterrupted show. All too often, teams pursuing adventurous and novel formations left the audience waiting for aircraft to reform and continue their performance. Though the 'Diamond Nine' had been flown previously by various teams, including The Black Arrows and The Blue Diamonds and several international teams, it was The Red Arrows who perfected it with ultra-close formation and who are most associated with the manoeuvre. *(RAF-T 8173)*

The RAF's first free-fall parachute display team was formed in 1961 by six parachute instructors of No. 1 Parachute Training School, RAF Abingdon. In 1965, following official recognition, the team enlarged to twelve men under Flight Lieutenant John Thirtle and adopted the name The Falcons. In May 1967, six of the Falcons jumped from an Argosy over RAF El Adem to create a six-man link-up, a new British record. Seen here prior to the jump, The Falcons were: leader Flight Lieutenant Stuart Cameron, Flight Sergeant Tony 'Geordie' Charlton and Sergeants Julian Tasker, David Jones, Ken Mapplebeck, and Brian Clark-Sutton. They were joined by Flight Sergeant Terence Allen, acting as photographer. As with all display teams, The Falcons' technique was honed and improved over the years. An advanced manoeuvre in British display parachuting at the time, a six-man link is a standard manoeuvre today. *(RAF-T 6888)*

The Falcons parachute display team has jumped from a number of different aircraft. Principally the Beverley, later replaced by the Argosy, but also the Hastings, Andover and a variety of helicopters were used. Seen here, at approximately 12,000ft, two Falcons have just jumped from Argosy XR139 and are in the process of getting control of their descent. Having jumped while facing forwards, they twisted their body to adopt a more stable position, usually with arms and legs spread out and an arched back. After just ten seconds freefall, parachutists reached speeds of approximately 120mph. After assembling, the team performed a series of manoeuvres consisting of links, stacks and their signature bomb burst. As during aircraft displays, parachute routines are accentuated by the use of smoke. Within two minutes the team had landed following the successful deployment of their parachutes at 2,000ft. (RAF-T 7012)

Not all RAF display teams used aircraft. First established in 1944, the principle role of RAF Police dog units was to provide airfield security. Soon after their introduction, the skill and technique of handling RAF Police dogs was recognized to benefit public relations. In 1948, The RAF Police Dog Demonstration Team was formed to perform at that year's Royal Tournament. Over subsequent years, the popular team demonstrated at events around Great Britain and the world. In this photograph, the team of 1958 is seen at the RAF Police Depot at Netheravon where it trained. In the foreground is Police Dog Handler Corporal J. Tait with 4686 Airdog Comet, the team's mascot for their tenth anniversary Royal Tournament appearance. That year, Airdog Comet led the thirty-four man team into the Earls Court arena. *(RAF-T 589)*

Index